MW00980832

WITHOUT HIM, WE CAN DO NOTHING

BY FRANCIS FRANGIPANE

All Scriptures NAS unless otherwise noted.

The vision of seeing our cities turned and revival coming to our land cannot be fulfilled without God. I know that sounds too simplistic, something we are sure we already know. But the fact is, the Stone which the builders rejected in the first century is the Stone of stumbling in our day as well.

Our lack of attention and consecration toward the Lord demonstrates that, although we know these things, we fail to live them. So, I will say it again: the will of God, no matter what that means to you, cannot be fulfilled apart from your daily love affair with Jesus Christ.

No matter what we think God wants us to do with our lives, knowing Jesus and loving Him *is* the life-spring of God's will for us. The scriptures tell us, **"all things are from Him and through Him and for Him" (Romans 11:36).** We may be called to accomplish many tasks in our lives, but only those deeds which have been truly wrought in Him are accepted by Him as fulfillment of His will. We must see that the will of God for us requires the presence and work of Jesus Himself. Apart from Him, we can do nothing.

Thus, we find the Holy Spirit directing us continually back to Jesus. Without Him, our prayers are just rituals. Apart from Him, our Christianity is but another empty religion. The focus of our hearts must be upon truly seeking the Lord Jesus Christ.

To Seek Him for Himself

When we contemplate seeking God, we usually must find reasons or problems to motivate us closer. Jesus is jealous for us to seek Him for Himself. He is looking for His BRIDE, not just someone who "dates" Him on weekends! He wants to live within us and possess our thoughts, literally making a home for Himself within our hearts. He does not care how skilled our minds are; *He just wants all the mind we have.*

You see, He *owns* us. By His sacrifice our ransom was paid. He alone rescued us from hell. He forgave us, cleansed us and became our very righteousness. He then translated us out of the dominion of darkness and brought us into His Kingdom, .

where He continues to sustain and love us. He gave His all; He deserves our all.

As we come closer to the end of this age, in an ever-increasing way the Lord Jesus Himself shall be exalted in His church. Speaking of the last days, Peter said, **"The end of all things is at hand…" (I Peter 4:7).** Programs, methods, gimmicks and hype will all fall uselessly to the ground; it will truly be an end to all *things.*

This is especially important for those of us who are Americans. For, by nature, we are an inventive and ingenious people. If we cannot accomplish our objective through one means, we simply try another approach. We are almost inexhaustible in our willingness to find different ways to conduct church, to appear Christian, to appeal to and attract people to our churches. Yet, even now, the Lord is drying up the things upon which we have relied. In this last, great day, the Lord alone shall be exalted!

Thus, He is calling us into a greater, more perfect dependency upon Him. It may seem like a difficult time, but this dependency is nothing less than God preparing the Bride for the return of the Lord Jesus.

To Be Known for Knowing Him

In our immaturity, the church has sought to be known for many things. We have sought to be known for our uniqueness and particular emphasis. Some sought to be known for speaking in tongues; others desired recognition through their buildings or evangelistic programs. Still others publicized unique combinations of church government or a regular agenda of special speakers.

Today's disciples, however, will be known for just one thing: *They will be known for truly knowing Jesus.* His presence, not just doctrines about Him, but His very Spirit and likeness, will uninhibitedly accompany those who follow the Lamb.

Because their focus is upon Him and Him alone, God will ultimately accompany their lives with great power. They will lay hands upon the sick and instantaneous healings will be common. Miracles, though, will be incidental. Their eyes will ever be upon Jesus.

When their hands are not being laid upon the sick, they will be lifted in worship. They will truly do the **"greater works"** spoken of in John 14:12, but they will not write books about *their* works, they will only talk about *His.*

Follow Paul's Example

The man who penned nearly half the New Testament never set out to write the books of the Bible. *His goal was to know Christ.* Paul said:

I count all things to be loss in view of the surpassing value of knowing Christ Jesus my Lord, for whom I have suffered the loss of all things, and count them but rubbish in order that I may gain Christ (Philippians 3:8).

Everything else in Paul's heart, all his personal attainments were incidental compared to his passion to know Jesus.

Paul continued:

Not that I have already obtained it, or have already become perfect, but I press on in order that I may lay hold of that for which also I was laid hold of by Christ Jesus.

Brethren, I do not regard myself as having laid hold of it yet; but one thing I do: forgetting what lies

behind and reaching forward to what lies ahead,

I press on toward the goal for the prize of the upward call of God in Christ Jesus (Philippians 3:12-14).

Does it amaze you that this apostle, who had *seen* the Lord Jesus, spent the rest of his life "pressing on" to lay hold of more of Christ? Paul could seemingly have stopped at any point and felt he had arrived. And as we read his epistles, his "arrival" could have been our goal. But no, his life was given to seeking after the Lord.

"Let us therefore, as many as are perfect, have this attitude; and if in anything you have a different attitude, God will reveal that also to you" (Philippians 3:15). He said, **"As many as are perfect [mature] have this attitude."** True spiritual maturity is not defined in how many people attend our churches, how many books we have written or what miracles accompany our lives. Spiritual development is seen in how consumed we have become with knowing and possessing the heart of Christ.

Paul continued, **"Brethren, join in following my example, and observe those who walk according to the pattern you have in us" (Philippians 3:17).** One of the major problems in Christianity today is that we have been following patterns set by men who have not exemplified these passions.

In many cases, we have found ourselves following individuals who have been good administrators, promoters and theologians yet have not had an insatiable hunger for God. We have turned Christianity into a history lesson instead of a love affair.

Paul said, **"Brethren [that's us] join in …my example."** The example to which he referred was one of seeking hard after God.

If our understanding of Christianity does not have this pattern, it is simply incomplete.

You see, we cannot rest on our initial meeting with the Lord. We must press on. There is something that, even now, Jesus is reaching to give to each of us, which we must, in return, reach to "lay hold of." That *something* is nothing less than Christ Himself.

"If in anything you have a different attitude, God will reveal that also to you" (verse 15). It is my prayer that if any of us has an attitude other than pressing on to know Jesus, that the Holy Spirit would reveal our hearts to us. Our only mindset should be that of seeking to know Him. Goals of looking to be blessed or prosperous are on too low a level.

Paul wrote, **"…for we are the true circumcision, who worship in the Spirit of God and glory in Christ Jesus and put no confidence in the flesh" (Philippians 3:3).** The true sign that you are following God is that you worship Him in Spirit, glory in Christ Jesus and that you put absolutely no confidence in the flesh.

Our salvation is not based upon what we do, but upon Who Jesus becomes to us. Christ alone is our righteousness, our virtue and our strength! As we minister, it has to be in Jesus' power or we are actually wasting time. Our confidence has to be in Him and not in our own abilities. We must be settled in the knowledge that, while all things are possible for those who believe, apart from Him, we can do nothing. He is the answer for our cities and the fulfillment of our hearts. ∎

Francis Frangipane is the founder of River of Life Ministries in Cedar Rapids, Iowa, and leads Advancing Church Ministries, which conducts conferences in various cities focusing on themes such as intercession and city-wide prayer movements, spiritual warfare, and unity in the church. He is the author of several books, including *The House of the Lord: God's Plan to Liberate Your City from Darkness, The Three Battlegrounds,* and *Holiness, Truth and the Presence of God.*

COMBATING THE RELIGIOUS SPIRIT

BY RICK JOYNER

All Scriptures NAS unless otherwise noted.

Loving God is the greatest commandment and the greatest gift that a man can possess. The second great commandment is to love our neighbor. As the Lord affirmed, the whole Law is fulfilled by keeping these two commandments. If we love the Lord we will not worship idols. If we love our neighbors we will not envy them, steal from them, or murder them, etc. Therefore, keeping these two positive commandments to love will enable us to fulfill all of the negative "do nots" of the Law.

Jack Deere once said, "Passion for the Son of God will conquer a thousand evils in our hearts, and is the most powerful weapon against evil in our lives." Because loving God is our highest goal it must be the primary focus of our lives. That is why one of the enemy's most deceptive and deadly attacks upon the church is meant to divert us from this ultimate quest. It is his strategy to keep us focused on the evil in our lives, knowing that we will become what we are beholding (see II Corinthians

3:18). As long as we keep looking at the evil it will continue to have dominion over us. When we look to the Lord and behold His glory, we are changed into His image.

This is not to imply that we excuse and overlook the sin and error in our lives. In fact the scriptures command us to examine ourselves and test ourselves to be sure that we are still in the faith. The issue is who do we turn to after iniquity is discovered? Do we turn to the Tree of the Knowledge of Good and Evil, or to the Tree of Life? Do we try to make ourselves better so that we will then be acceptable to God, or do we turn to the cross of Jesus to find both the forgiveness and the power to overcome the sin?

A primary strategy of the enemy is intended to keep us focused on the evil, partaking of the Tree of Knowledge, and away from the glory of the Lord and the cross. This tactic comes in the form of a *religious spirit*. This spirit is the counterfeit to the true love of God, and true worship. This evil spirit has done far more damage to the church than anything the New Age

Movement, and all of the other cults combined have been able to accomplish.

The Nature of a Religious Spirit

A religious spirit is a demon which seeks to substitute religious activity for the power of the Holy Spirit in the believer's life. Its primary objective is to have the church **"holding to a form of godliness, although they have denied its power**... **(II Timothy 3:5).** The apostle completes his exhortation with **"avoid such men as these."** This religious spirit is the **"leaven of the Pharisees and Sadducees" (Matthew 16:6)** of which the Lord warned His disciples to beware.

When the Lord used metaphors it was because their characteristics were similar to the object of the lesson. The religious spirit does operate like leaven in bread. It does not add substance or nutritional value to the bread, it only inflates it. Such is the result of the religious spirit. It does not add to the life and power of the church, it feeds the very pride of man which caused the first fall, and almost every one since. Satan probably understands even better than the church that **"God resists the proud, but gives grace to the humble" (James 4:6).** He knows very well that God will not inhabit any work that he can inflate through pride, and will even resist it Himself.

Satan also knows that once leaven gets into the bread, it is most difficult to remove. Pride, by its very nature, is the most difficult stronghold to correct or remove. A religious spirit keeps us from hearing the voice of God by having us assume that we already know God's opinion, what He is saying, and what pleases Him. This delusion is the result of believing that God is just like us. This will cause even the rationalization of Scripture, having us believe that rebukes, exhortations and words of correction are for other people, not us.

In fact, if this is a problem in your life you have probably already begun to think about how badly someone you know needs to read this. It may not even have occurred to you that God put this into your hands because *you* need it. In fact, we all need it. This is one issue that each of us is probably battling to some degree. It is imperative that we get free of this devastating deception, and stay free. We will not be able to fully worship the Lord in Spirit and truth until we do.

The degree to which we are able to preach the true gospel in true power is determined by the degree to which we have been delivered from this most powerful and destructive deception. The church's confrontation with the religious spirit will be one of the epic battles of the last days. Everyone will be fighting in this battle. The only issue to be determined is which side we will be on during this battle.

We will not have the authority to deliver others from darkness if we are not free ourselves. To begin taking ground from this vast enemy, let us ask the Lord to shine His light to show how this applies to us! As the Lord's continuous confrontations with the Pharisees were an example, the church's most desperate fight from the very beginning has been with this spirit. Just as the primary characteristic of the Pharisees was their tendency to see what was wrong with others, while not being able to see their own faults, the religious spirit tries to make us more prone to seeing what is wrong with others than the need for our own correction.

The Great Deception

One of the most deceptive characteristics about the religious spirit is that it is founded upon zeal for God. We tend to think that zeal for God cannot be evil, but that depends on *why* we are zealous for Him. As Paul wrote of his Jewish brethren in Romans 10:2, **"I bear them witness that they have a *zeal* for God, but not in accordance with knowledge."** No one on earth prayed more, fasted more, read the Bible more, had a greater hope in the coming of the Messiah, or had more zeal for the things of God, than the Pharisees—yet they were the greatest opposers of God and His Messiah when He came. In fact, the young Saul of Tarsus was motivated by zeal for God while he was persecuting the church.

The Lord had little trouble with demons while He walked the earth. They would quickly bow the knee to Him and beg for mercy. It was the conservative, zealous, religious community that immediately became His greatest enemy. Those who were the most zealous for the word of God crucified the Word when He appeared to walk among them. The same is still true. All of the cults and false religions combined have not done as much damage to the moves of God as the opposition or infiltration of the religious spirit. Cults and false religions are easily discerned, but the religious spirit has thwarted or diverted possibly every revival or movement to date, and it still retains a seat of honor throughout most of the visible church. It is a manifestation of the religious spirit that will take his seat in the very temple of God (which is the church), declaring himself to be God, and getting almost the whole world to follow him.

The Two Foundations

Like most of the enemy's powerful strongholds, the religious spirit builds its work on two basic foundations—fear and pride. *The religious spirit seeks to have us serve the Lord in order to gain His approval, rather than from a position of having our approval through the cross of Jesus.* Therefore the religious spirit bases its relationship to God on personal discipline rather than the propitious sacrifice of Christ. The motivation for doing this can be either fear or pride, or a combination of both.

Fear and pride are the two basic results of the fall, and our deliverance from them is usually a long process. That is why the Lord gave even Jezebel "time to repent" (see Revelation 2:20,21). The biblical Jezebel was the wife of King Ahab and a very religious woman, but one who was given to false religion. The Lord gave her time to repent because the roots of this spirit go so deep that it takes time to repent and be delivered from it.

However, even though the Lord gave Jezebel time to repent, He rebuked the church of Thyatira for "tolerating" her (verse 20). We can be patient with people who have religious spirits, giving them time to repent, but we must not tolerate their ministry in our midst while we're waiting! If this spirit is not confronted quickly it will do more damage to the church, our ministries, our families, and our lives, than possibly any other assault that we can suffer.

The Foundation of Guilt

Eli, the priest who raised Samuel, is a good biblical example of someone who ministers in a religious spirit founded upon guilt. Eli had so much zeal for the Lord that when he heard that the Ark had been captured by the Philistines he fell over and died. He had spent his life trying to serve the Lord as the High Priest, but the very first word given to Samuel was one of the most frightening rebukes given in the Scriptures—for Eli!

For I have told him that I am about to judge his house forever for the iniquity which he knew, because his sons brought a curse on themselves and he did not rebuke them.

And therefore I have sworn to the house of Eli that the iniquity of Eli's house shall not be atoned for by sacrifice or offering forever (I Samuel 3:13, 14).

Eli's zeal for the Lord was based on sacrifices and offerings intended to compensate for his irresponsibility as a father. Guilt in our lives can stir us on to great zeal for the Lord, which usually results in our attempt to use sacrifices and offerings as an atonement for our failings. This is an affront to the cross, which alone can atone for our guilt. Such zeal will never be acceptable to the Lord, even if we can make sacrifices forever.

We should note here that the Lord did not say that Eli's sin could not be forgiven. He just said that Eli's attempts to atone for sin by sacrifice and offering would never atone for it. There are multitudes of men and women whose zeal for the Lord is likewise based on an attempt to atone for sins, failures, or irresponsibility in other areas of their lives.

This opens the door wide for a religious spirit because the service is not based on the blood of Jesus and the power of the cross, but an attempt to make our own atonement for sin. Again, any attempt to perform ministry in order to gain God's approval is an affront to the cross by which alone we can be approved. This does not mean that we do not do things to please the Lord, but we must keep as our motive pleasing the Lord for *His* joy, not for our acceptance. One is God-centered, and the other is self-centered, and that of the most destructive kind—an attempt to circumvent the cross.

It is also noteworthy that one of the sins of Eli's sons was that they **"despised the offering of the Lord" (I Samuel 2:17).** They appropriated the sacrifices and offerings brought to the Lord for their own selfish use. Those who are gripped by this form of a religious spirit will often be the most zealous to preach the cross, but theirs is a perversion in that it emphasizes *their* cross more than the cross of Jesus. Their delight really is more in self-abasement, than in the cross of Christ which alone makes us righteous and acceptable to God.

The Foundation of Pride

Idealism is one of the most deceptive and destructive disguises of the religious spirit. Idealism is of human origin and is a form of humanism. It has the appearance of only seeking the highest standards and the preservation of God's glory. However, idealism is possibly the most deadly enemy of true revelation and true grace. It is deadly because it does not allow for growing up into grace and wisdom, but attacks and destroys the foundation of those who are in pursuit of God's glory, but are not there yet.

Idealism tries to impose standards on others that is beyond what God has required, or has given grace for. Men controlled by this kind of religious spirit may condemn as unspiritual anyone who is not praying two hours a day as they are. The grace of God may want us to pray two hours a day, but He will first call us to pray ten minutes a day. Then, as we become so blessed by His presence, we will want to spend more and more time with Him until we will not want to quit after ten minutes, then an hour, then two.

A religious spirit based on idealism will always be seeking the perfect church and refuse to be a part of anything less. Those led by the Holy Spirit may have hopes for a church that are just as high, but can still give themselves in service to even some of the most lowly works in order to help them grow in vision and maturity. The Holy Spirit is called "the Helper," and those who are truly led by the Spirit will always be looking for ways to help, not just stand aloof and criticize.

When a religious spirit is founded upon pride it is evidenced by *perfectionism*. The perfectionist sees everything as black or white. This develops into extremes as it requires that everyone and every teaching be judged as either 100% right or 100% wrong. This is a standard that only Jesus could comply with and leads to a serious delusion when we impose it on ourselves or others. True grace imparts a truth that sets us free, showing us the way out of our sin, or to higher levels of spiritual maturity.

One with a religious spirit can usually point to problems with great accuracy, but usually offers no solutions, except to tear down what has already been built. This is the strategy of the enemy to nullify progress that has already been made, and to bring about a discouragement that will limit future progress. This produces the mentality that, if we cannot go straight to the top of the mountain, we should not climb at all, but just "die to self." This is a

death that God has not required, and is a perversion of the exhortation for us to take up our crosses daily.

The grace of God will lead us up the mountain step by step. The Lord does not condemn us because we may trip a few times while trying to climb. He graciously picks us up and encourages us that we can make it. We must have a vision of making it to the top, and should never condemn ourselves for not being there yet, *as long as we are still climbing.* As James said, "We all stumble in many ways." If we had to wait until we were perfect before we could minister, no one would ever qualify for the ministry. Perfect obedience and understanding should always be our goal, but such will never be found within ourselves, but only as we come to perfectly abide in the Perfect One.

Because we now "see through a glass darkly," or in part, we are compelled to always be open to greater accuracy in our beliefs and teachings. One of the greatest delusions of all is that we are already complete in our understanding, or 100% accurate in our perception or actions. This closes us to further understanding and correction. The perfectionist both imposes and tries to live by standards that stifle true maturity and growth.

Jesus blessed Peter and turned the keys of the kingdom over to him just before He had to rebuke him and call him "Satan" (see Matthew 16:23). Right after this greatest of blessings the enemy deceived him, yet the Lord did not take the keys away from Peter. Jesus knew when He gave the keys to Peter that he was soon to even deny that he knew Him. Many years after Peter used the keys to open the door of faith for both the Jews and Gentiles, the youngest of the apostles had to rebuke him publicly because of his hypocrisy. Even so, Peter was promised to sit on one of the twelve thrones judging the twelve tribes of Israel.

It seems that the Lord's leadership style was to provide a place where his followers could make mistakes and learn from them. I know that if I required my children to be perfectly mature now it would be counter-productive, actually stifling their growth and maturity. The same is true in the church. We must bring correction for mistakes, because that is how we learn, but it must be a correction that encourages and frees, not one that condemns and crushes initiative.

Both Foundations

One of the most powerful and deceptive forms of the religious spirit is built upon *both* foundations of fear and pride. Those who are bound in this way will go through periods of deep anguish and remorse at their failures, resulting in a repentance that is simply more self-abasement producing more sacrifices in an attempt to appease the Lord. Then they will flip to the other side where they become so convinced that they are superior to other Christians, other groups, movements, etc. that they become unteachable and unable to receive reproof.

Such a religious spirit is so slippery that it will wiggle out of almost any attempt to confront it. If you address the pride, the fears and insecurities will rise up to attract sympathy. If you confront the fear it will then change into religious pride masquerading as faith. This type of spirit will drive individuals or congregations to such extremes that they will inevitably disintegrate.

The Counterfeit Gift of Discernment

A religious spirit gives birth to a counterfeit gift of discernment of spirits. This counterfeit gift thrives on seeing what is wrong with others rather than seeing what God is doing in order to help them along. This is where this spirit does some of its greatest damage in the church. Its ministry will almost always leave more damage and division than healing and reconciliation. Its wisdom is rooted in the Tree of the Knowledge of Good and Evil, and though the truth may be accurate, it is ministered in a spirit that kills.

This counterfeit gift of discernment is motivated by suspicion and fear. The suspicion is rooted in such things as rejection, territorial preservation, or general insecurity. The true gift of discernment can only function with love. Any motive other than love will distort spiritual perception. Whenever someone submits a judgment or criticism about another person or group, I disregard it unless I know that the one bringing it truly loves that person or group, and has an "investment" of service to them.

Angels of Light

When Paul warned the Corinthians about those who ministered in a religious spirit, which sought to bring a yoke of legalism upon the young church, he explained that:

> **… such men are false apostles, deceitful workers, disguising themselves as apostles of Christ.**

> **And no wonder, for even Satan disguises himself as an angel of light.**

Therefore it is not surprising if his servants also disguise themselves as servants of righteousness… **(II Corinthians 11:13-15).**

That Satan disguises himself as an "angel of light" could be interpreted as a "messenger of truth." Satan's most deceptive, and deadly, disguise is to come as a servant of righteousness, using truths for the purpose of destruction. He is quite adept at quoting Scripture, and using wisdom, but it is the wisdom of the Tree of Knowledge that kills. He can accurately point out what is wrong with someone else, but he always does it in such a way that tears down, not offering solutions that lead to deliverance and life.

"Angels of light" who are empowered by a religious spirit will have the mentality of first looking for what is wrong with someone rather than what is right. The guise will usually be the protection of the sheep, or the Lord's glory, but a critical spirit is an evil spirit and will always end up causing division and destruction. Criticism holds forth an appearance of wisdom, but criticism is pride in one of its most base forms. When we criticize someone else we are by that declaring ourselves to be better than they are. We may be better than others in some areas, but if we are, it is only by grace. One who knows the true grace of God never looks at how to put others down, but how to build them up, using the same grace upon which they have built their lives. As an old proverb declares, "Any jackass can kick a barn down, but it requires a skillful carpenter to build one."

The Religious Spirit and Murder

When Adam and Eve determined to live by the Knowledge of Good and Evil they were partaking of the religious spirit. The first result of this was self-centeredness —they looked at themselves. The first child born to them after partaking of this fruit was Cain, who is the first biblical model of one controlled by the religious spirit.

Cain was "a tiller of the ground," or earthly minded. The religious spirit will always seek to have us focused on the earthly realm rather than the heavenly realm. This "seed of Cain" judges by what it sees, and cannot understand those who "endure by seeing Him who is unseen." In Revelation we see the first beast **"coming up out of the earth" (Revelation 13:11)**; it is the result of the seed of Cain being tillers of the ground. This earthly mindedness has produced one of the most evil beasts the world will ever know.

Cain also tried to make an offering to the Lord from his own labors. God rejected that sacrifice, but accepted Abel's sacrifice of the blood. The fruit of our labors will never be an acceptable offering to the Lord. This was a statement from the very beginning that God would only accept the blood of the Lamb. Instead of receiving this correction and repenting, Cain became jealous of his brother, and slew him. Those who attempt to live by their own works will often become enraged at those who take their stand on the righteousness of the Lamb.

That is why Saul of Tarsus, the "Pharisee of Pharisees" was so enraged against the church. They represented the greatest threat to what the Pharisees had built their whole lives on. Their very existence could not be endured. Religions that are based on works will tend to become violent very easily. This includes "Christian" religions where a doctrine of works has supplanted the cross of Christ.

The Lord said that if a man just hates his brother he is guilty of murder. Those who are driven by religious spirits may try to destroy by other means than physically taking lives. Many of the onslaughts of slander instigated against churches and ministries are the ragings of this same religious spirit that caused Cain to slay his brother.

The Test of a True Messenger

In Ezekiel 37 the prophet was taken to a valley full of dry bones and asked if they could live. The Lord then commanded him to "prophesy to these bones." As he prophesied they came together, came to life, and then became a great army. This is a test which every true ministry must pass. The true prophet can see a great army in even the driest of bones. He will prophesy life to those bones until they come to life, and then become an army. A false prophet with a religious spirit will do little more than just tell the bones how dry they are, heaping discouragement and condemnation on them, but giving no life or power to overcome their circumstances.

Apostles and prophets are given authority to build up and tear down, but we have no right to tear down if we have not first built up. I will give no one the authority to bring correction to the people under my care unless they have a history of feeding them and building them up. You may say that eliminates the ministry of the "prophets," but I say that those "prophets" need to be eliminated from ministry. As Jude said of them, **"These men are grumblers, fault-finders…"** who are **"hidden reefs in your love feasts"** (see Jude 11-16).

Even so, as Eli gave us an example, woe to the shepherds who feed and care for the sheep but fail to correct them. The true grace of God is found between the extremes of the spirits of fault finding and unsanctified mercy (showing mercy to the things that God disapproves of). Either extreme can be the result of a religious spirit.

Jezebel

The spirit of Jezebel is another form of the religious spirit. Jezebel was the ambitious and manipulative wife of King Ahab, a weak leader who allowed her to dictate policy in his kingdom. It should be noted that Jezebel **"calls herself a prophetess" (Revelation 2:20).** This is often one of the telltale signs of false prophets who are operating in a religious spirit—they are preoccupied with their own recognition as a prophet, or prophetess. Our ministry is corrupted to the degree that self-seeking and the need for recognition abides within us. One who is easily offended because he is not received by a title or claim to position should never be accepted by that title or given that position!

The difference between the one who is motivated by a desire for acceptance or recognition, rather than love for the Lord and union with His purposes, is the difference between the false prophet and the true. The Lord Himself declared:

> He who speaks from himself seeks his own glory [literal: "recognition"]; but He who is seeking the glory of the one who sent Him, He is true, and there is no unrighteousness in Him (John 7:18).

Jezebel demands recognition for herself while serving as the enemy of the true prophetic ministry. Jezebel was the greatest enemy of one of the Old Covenant's most powerful prophets, Elijah, whose ministry especially represents the preparing of the way for the Lord. The Jezebel spirit is also one of the enemy's most potent forms of the religious spirit which seeks to keep the church and the world from being prepared for the return of the Lord. This spirit attacks the prophetic ministry because that has always been a primary way in which the Lord gives timely, strategic direction to His people. She knows that by removing the true prophets, the people will be vulnerable to her false prophets, which always leads to idolatry and spiritual adultery.

When there is a void of hearing the true voice of the Lord, the people will be much more prone to the deception of the enemy. This is why the enemy always tries to sow pride into the people. A religious spirit produces religious pride so that God will not speak to them. This is why Jesus calls the religious leaders of His own day "blind guides." These men, who knew the messianic prophecies better than anyone else in the world, could look right into the face of the One who was the fulfillment of those prophecies and think that He was sent from Beelzebub.

Jezebel's prophets of Baal were also given to sacrifice, even being willing to flail and cut themselves seeking the manifestation of their god. A primary strategy of the religious spirit is to get the church devoted to sacrifice in a way that perverts the command for us to take up our crosses daily. This perversion will have us putting more faith in our sacrifices than in the Lord's sacrifice. It will also use sacrifices and offerings to get God to manifest Himself. This is a form of the terrible delusion that we can somehow purchase the grace and presence of God with our good works.

Root of Self-Righteousness

We do not crucify ourselves for the sake of righteousness, purification, spiritual maturity, or to get the Lord to manifest Himself; this is nothing less than conjuring. We are **"crucified with Christ" (Galatians 2:20).** If we "crucify ourselves" it will only result in *self-righteousness*. This is pride in its most base form and is an affront to the cross of Jesus as well. It is pride in a most deceptive form because it gives the appearance of wisdom and righteousness. The Apostle Paul warned:

Let no one keep defrauding you of your prize by delighting in self-abasement and the worship of the angels, taking his stand on visions he has seen, inflated without cause by his fleshly mind,

and not holding fast to the head, from whom the entire body, being supplied and held together by the joints and ligaments, grows with a growth which is from God.

If you have died with Christ to the elementary principles of the world, why, as if you were living in the world, do you submit yourself to decrees, such as,

"Do not handle, do not taste, do not touch!"

(which all refer to things destined to perish with the using)—in accordance with the commandments and teachings of men?

These are matters which have, to be sure, the appearance of wisdom in self-made religion and self-abasement and severe treatment of the body, but are of no value

against fleshly indulgence (Colossians 2:18-23).

The religious spirit will make us feel very good about our spiritual condition as long as it is self-centered and self-seeking. Pride feels good; it can even be exhilarating. But it has all of our attention on how well we are doing, on how we stand compared to others—not on the glory of God. This results in our putting confidence in discipline and personal sacrifice rather than in the Lord and His sacrifice.

Of course discipline and the commitment to self-sacrifice are essential qualities for every believer to have, but it is the motivation behind them that determines whether we are being driven by a religious spirit, or by the Holy Spirit. A religious spirit motivates through fear, guilt, or pride and ambition. The motivation of the Holy Spirit is love for the Son of God.

Delighting in self-abasement is a sure symptom of the religious spirit. This does not mean that we do not discipline ourselves, fast, or buffet our bodies as Paul did. It is the perverted delighting in this, rather than in the Son of God, that reveals a problem.

Deceptive Revelation

Colossians 2:18, 19, explains that a man with a religious spirit that delights in self-abasement will often also be given to worshiping angels and taking improper stands on visions they have seen. A religious spirit wants us to worship anything or anyone but Jesus. The same spirit that is given to worshiping angels will also be prone to excessively exalt men. We must beware of anyone who unduly exalts angels, men or women of God, or uses visions they have received to gain improper influence in the church. God does not give us revelations so that people will respect us more, or to prove our ministry. The fruit of true revelation will be humility, not pride. The Scriptures teach that Christians do have these experiences, and that they are useful and needed when used properly. The key word in this text is that we should beware of those who are having such revelations *and* are being "inflated," by them.

A religious spirit will always feed our pride; whereas true spiritual maturity will always lead to increasing humility. This progression of humility is wonderfully demonstrated in the life of Paul the apostle. In his letter to the Galatians, estimated to have been written in A.D. 56, he declares that when he visited the original apostles in Jerusalem, they **"added nothing to me"** **(2:6 KJV).** In a sense he was declaring that he had as much as they did. In his first letter to the Corinthians, written about six years later, he calls himself the **"least of the apostles" (15:9).** In his letter to Ephesians, written in about A.D. 61, he declares himself to be **"the very least of all saints" (3:8).** When writing to Timothy in approximately A.D. 65 he declared himself to be the **"chief of sinners" (I Timothy 1:15),** adding that God had mercy on him. *A true revelation of God's mercy is the greatest antidote for the religious spirit.*

The Martyr Syndrome

The martyr syndrome is one of the ultimate and most deadly delusions when combined with the religious spirit. To be a true martyr for the faith is one of the greatest honors that we can receive in this life. When this is perverted it is a tragic form of deception. When a religious spirit is combined with the martyr syndrome it is almost impossible for that person to be delivered from his deception. At that point any rejection or correction is perceived as the price he must bear to "stand for the truth." This will drive him even further from the truth and any possibility of correction.

The martyr syndrome can also be a form of the spirit of suicide. It is sometimes much easier to "die for the Lord," than it is to live for Him. Those who have a perverted understanding of the cross glory more in death than they do in life. The point of the cross is the resurrection, not the grave.

Self-help Psychology

There is a "self-help psychology" movement that is attempting to replace the power of the cross in the church. Humanistically based psychology is "another gospel;" it is an enemy of the cross, and another form of the religious spirit. Indeed Paul warned us:

As you therefore have received Christ Jesus the Lord, so walk in Him,

having been firmly rooted and now being built up in Him and established in your faith, just as you were instructed, and overflowing with gratitude.

See to it that no one takes you captive through philosophy and empty deception, according to the tradition of men, according to the elementary principles of the world, rather than according to Christ (Colossians 2:6-8)

We all need "inner healing" to some degree, but much of what is being called inner healing is nothing less than digging up the old man and trying to get him healed. The answer to these deep wounds

is not a procedure or formula, but simple forgiveness. When we go to the cross and find true acceptance, based on the blood of Jesus, we will find a perfect love able to cast out all of our fears, and wash away all bitterness and resentment.

This seems too simple, but that is why Paul said: **"But I am afraid, lest as the serpent deceived Eve by his craftiness, your minds should be led astray from the simplicity and purity of devotion to Christ (II Corinthians 11:3).** Salvation is simple. Deliverance is simple. There is a major strategy of the enemy to dilute the power of the gospel by having us add to it, which is how Eve was deceived.

The Lord had commanded the man and woman not to eat from the Tree of the Knowledge of Good and Evil because they would die. When asked about this command Eve replied that they could not eat from the tree *"or touch it"* (see Genesis 3:3). The Lord had not said anything about not touching the tree. Adding to the commandments is just as destructive as taking away from them—anyone who thinks that they can so flippantly add to the word of God does not respect it enough to keep it when the testing comes. If Satan can get us to add or subtract from it, he then knows he has us just like he did Eve.

There are many "Christian" philosophies and therapies that seem wise, but are in fact attempting to be substitutes for the Holy Spirit in our lives. Some people do need counseling, and there are many Christian counselors who do lead people to the cross. Others are simply leading people into a black hole of self-centeredness that will consume them and try to suck in everyone else around them too. In spite of the Christian terminology, this philosophy is an enemy of the cross of Christ.

Summary

Basically the religious spirit seeks to replace the Holy Spirit as our source of spiritual life. It does this by seeking to replace true repentance that leads to grace by a repentance based on our performance. This replaces true humility with pride.

True religion is based on loving the Lord and then loving our neighbors. True religion will have discipline and obedience, but these are founded on love for the Lord rather than the desire for recognition or acceptance. The wife who keeps herself in shape because she loves her husband will be easily distinguished from the one who does it because of her own ego. The former will carry beauty with grace and dignity; the latter may be appealing, but it will be a seductive appeal that is a perversion of true love.

The religious spirit is basically a manifestation of the "good" side of the Tree of the Knowledge of Good and Evil. When Adam and Eve ate of that Tree in the Garden, the first result was that they looked at themselves. Self-centeredness is the poison that made that fruit deadly, and it is still the most deadly poison the serpent seeks to give us. The Holy Spirit will always lead us into a life that is Christ-centered. The religious spirit will have us focus our attention on ourselves by seeking to base our concept of the Christian life on performance.

The Holy Spirit produces fruit by joining us to the Lord. **"For the word of the cross is to those who are perishing foolishness, but to us who are being saved it is the power of God"** (I Corinthians 1:18). However, we must understand that this is the cross of Christ, not our own crosses. We are called to deny ourselves and take up our crosses daily, but we do not glory in or try to live by the power of our own sacrifices, or by "delighting in self-abasement." We glory in what Jesus accomplished and the sacrifice that He made. We have our standing before God on the basis of His cross. Our ability to come boldly before the throne of God has nothing to do with whether we have had a good day or a bad day, or how well we have properly performed all of our religious duties. Our acceptance before God is based on one thing only—the sacrifice that Jesus made for our justification.

This does not negate the need for personal holiness, as James asserted, **"... faith without works is dead"** (James 2:26). If we are joined to Christ we will not go on living in sin. We do not become free of sin in order to abide in Him, but by abiding in Him. Jesus is the Way, the Truth and the Life. If He is not our Life then we do not really know the Way or the Truth either. It is the religious spirit that tries to keep Christianity in the realm of the Way and Truth while keeping us from the essential union by which Jesus becomes our Life. True Christianity does not just involve what we believe, but Who we believe.

True worship does not come in order to see the Lord, but it comes from seeing the Lord. When we see Him we will worship. When we see His glory we will no longer be so captivated by our own positive or negative qualities—our souls will be captured by His beauty. When the Lamb enters even the twenty-four elders cast their crowns at His feet (see Revelation 4:10). That is the goal of the true faith—to see Him, to abide in Him, and to reveal Him.

The world is becoming increasingly repulsed by religion. However, when Jesus is lifted up all men will be drawn to Him. Because the whole creation was created through Him and for Him, we all have a huge, Jesus-size, hole in our soul. Nothing else will ever satisfy us or bring us peace but a genuine relationship with Him.

When we are truly joined to Jesus, living water begins to flow out of our innermost being that cannot be stopped. As more and more are freed and this water begins to flow, it will become a great river of life in the midst of the earth. Those who drink from this river will never thirst again— they will have found satisfaction for the deepest yearning of the human soul. The more that we get free of this religious spirit the purer and clearer these waters will be.

Some Warning Signs of a Religious Spirit

1) *The tendency to see our primary mission as tearing down what we believe is wrong.* Such a person's ministry will produce more division and tearing down than lasting works that have been built and are bearing fruit for the kingdom.

2) *The inability to take a rebuke, especially from those we may judge to be less spiritual than ourselves.* Think back on how you responded the last few times someone tried to correct you.

3) *A philosophy that will not listen to men, but "only to God."* Since God usually speaks through men, this is an obvious delusion, and reveals serious spiritual pride.

4) *The inclination to see more of what is wrong with other people, other churches, etc., than what is right with them.* John saw Babylon from the valley, but when he was carried to "a high mountain" he saw the New Jerusalem. If we are only seeing Babylon it is because of our perspective. Those who are in a place of true vision will have their attention on what God is doing, not men.

5) *Overwhelming guilt that we can never measure up to the Lord's standards.* This is a root of the religious spirit because it causes us to base our relationship to Him on our performance rather than on the cross. Jesus has already measured up for us; He is the completed work that the Father is seeking to accomplish within us. Our whole goal in life should be simply to abide in Him.

6) *The belief that we have been appointed to fix everyone else.* These become the self-appointed watchmen, or sheriffs, in God's kingdom. These are seldom involved in building, but serve to only keep the church in a state of annoyance and agitation, if not causing serious divisions.

7) *A leadership style which is bossy, overbearing, and intolerant of the weakness or failure of others.* As James said:

"But the wisdom from above is first pure, then peaceable, gentle, reasonable, full of mercy and good fruits, unwavering, without hypocrisy.

And the seed whose fruit is righteousness is sown in peace by those who make peace" (James 3:17, 18).

8) *A sense that we are closer to God than other people, or that our lives or ministries are more pleasing to Him.* This is a symptom of the profound delusion that we draw closer to God by who we are rather than through Jesus.

9) *Pride in our spiritual maturity or discipline, especially as we compare to others.* True spiritual maturity involves growing up into Christ. When we begin to compare ourselves with others it is obvious that we have lost sight of the true goal— Jesus.

10) *The belief that we are on the cutting edge of what God is doing.* This would also include thinking that we are involved in the most important thing that God is doing.

11) *A mechanical prayer life.* When we start feeling relief when our prayer time is over, or we have prayed through our prayer list, we should consider our condition. You will never feel relief when your conversation is over with the one you love.

12) *Doing things in order to be noticed by men.* This is a symptom of the idolatry of fearing men more than we fear God, and results in a religion that serves men instead of God.

13) *Being overly repulsed by emotionalism.* When a person who is subject to a religious spirit encounters the true life of God it will usually appear excessive, emotional and carnal to them. True passion for God is emotional and demonstrative, such as David demonstrated when he brought the ark of God into Jerusalem.

14) *Using emotionalism as a substitute for the work of the Holy Spirit.* This would include such things as requiring weeping and wailing as evidence of repentance, or "falling under the power" as evidence that one has been touched by God. Both of these can be evidences of the true work of the Holy Spirit; it is when we require these manifestations that we are beginning to move in another spirit.

In the First Great Awakening, Jonathan Edwards' meetings would often have some of the toughest, most rebellious men falling on the ground and staying there for up to 24 hours. They got up changed, and such seemingly strange manifestations of the Holy Spirit fueled the Great Awakenings. Even so, Edwards stated that he believed that men faking the manifestations worked more to bring an end to the Great Awakening than the enemies of the revival.

15) *Keeping score on our spiritual lives.* This includes feeling better about ourselves because we go to more meetings, read our Bibles more, do more things for the Lord, etc. These are all noble endeavors, but the true measure of spiritual maturity is getting closer to the Lord.

16) *Being encouraged when our ministry looks better than others.* We could include in this being discouraged when it seems that others are looking better, or growing faster than we are.

17) *Glorying more in what God has done in the past than in the present.* God has not changed; He is the same yesterday, today and forever. The veil has been removed; we can be as close to God today as anyone ever has been in the past. A religious spirit always seeks to focus our attention on works, and making comparisons rather than simply drawing closer to the Lord.

18) *The tendency to be suspicious of, or to oppose new movements, churches, etc.* This is an obvious symptom of jealousy, a primary fruit of the religious spirit, or the pride that asserts that God would not do anything new without going through us. Of course, those with such a mentality are seldom used by the Lord to birth new works.

19) *The tendency to reject spiritual manifestations that we do not understand.* This is a symptom of pride and arrogance that presumes our opinions are the same as God's. True humility keeps us teachable and open, patiently waiting for fruit before making judgments. True discernment enables us to look for and hope for the best, not the worst. That is why we are exhorted to **"Prove all things, hold fast to what is good [not what is bad]" (I Thessalonians 5:21).**

20) *The overreaction to carnality in the church.* The truth is that there is probably far more carnality in the church, and a lot less of the Holy Spirit, than even the most critical person has seen. It is important that we learn to discern between them, be delivered from our carnality, and to grow in our submission to the Holy Spirit. But the critical person will want to annihilate those who may still be 60% carnal, but were 95% last year and are making progress, instead of helping them along the way.

21) *The overreaction to immaturity in the church.* There is a certain amount of immaturity that is tolerable with the Lord. My two year old is immature compared to my nine year old, but that is okay. In fact, he may be very mature for a two year old. The idealistic religious spirit only sees the immaturity without considering the other important factors.

22) *Being overly prone to base evidence of God's approval on manifestations.* This is just another form of keeping score and comparing ourselves to others. Jesus did some of His greatest miracles, such as walking on water, to be seen by only a few. He was doing His works to glorify the Father, not Himself. Those who use the evidence of miracles to testify and build their own ministries and reputations have made a serious departure from the path of life.

23) *The inability to join anything that they do not deem as being perfect or near perfect.* The Lord joined and even gave His life for the fallen human race. Such is the nature of those who abide in Him.

24) *Becoming overly paranoid of the religious spirit.* We do not get free of something by fearing it, but by overcoming it with faith in Christ Jesus.

25) *The tendency to glory in anything but the cross of Jesus, what He has* accomplished and Who He is. If we are building our lives, ministries, or churches on anything but these, we are building on a shaky foundation that will not stand.

Scoring on the Test

We are probably all subject to the religious spirit to at least some degree. Paul exhorts us to **"Test yourselves to see if you are in the faith" (II Corinthians 13:5).** First, He does not tell us to "test your neighbor," or to "test your pastor," but "yourselves." Using this to measure others by can be a symptom that we have a serious problem. If this article has given you illumination about another ministry, which is causing serious problems, be sure that you use it in the Holy Spirit. Let us heed the warning to the Galatians:

> **Brethren, even if a man is caught** *in any trespass***, you who are spiritual, restore such a one in a spirit of gentleness; each one looking to yourself, lest you too be tempted (Galatians 6:1).**

Special Acknowledgement

Some of the material for this article, as well as a few of the questions at the end, were derived from Jack Deere's outstanding tape series *Exposing The Religious Spirit*, which is available through the Tape Catalog of MorningStar Publications. ∎

Rick Joyner is the Executive Director of MorningStar Publications and is the Editor of The Morning Star Journal and The Morning Star Prophetic Bulletin. He is the author of several books including: *The Harvest, There Were Two Trees in the Garden, The Passover, Leadership, Management and the Five Essentials for Success, The Journey Begins, The World Aflame, Visions of the Harvest,* and his most recent release, *The Harvest Volume II.* Rick and his wife Julie have three daughters, Anna, Aaryn and Amber, and one son, Ben. They live in Charlotte, NC.

SWIFTER THAN EAGLES, STRONGER THAN LIONS

BY BONNIE CHAVDA

I n recent months the church world-wide has begun to receive the former rain of the Holy Spirit on our dry places. We are experiencing Pentecost in much of its original form and power. The Lord is moving again! However, just as when the Lord walked on the earth in the flesh, His movement agitates and reveals those who live by another spirit.

Jesus often said to His disciples, "Beware the leaven of the Pharisees." The Pharisees were puffed up in the knowledge of their own minds; they put more confidence in their own righteousness than they placed in the One who was sent to become our righteousness. The Lord's presence and authority threatened them, so they threatened Him.

In Matthew 12:22-37, we find the account of an event of increasing relevance to the modern church. This is a modern paraphrase of Jesus' discourse:

The Pharisees witness Jesus casting out an evil spirit and the subsequent healing of a man who had been blind and mute. The people witness Jesus' power and say, "This must be the king from David's lineage who is to restore the kingdom to us!" As this question is put to the Pharisees, they turn murderous with jealousy and reply, "Of course not. He is from the prince of darkness! Continue following us!" Jesus confronts them, "Every kingdom divided against itself will not stand. There is only One who can drive out demons—the Holy Spirit of God! He who is not with Me is against Me; He who does not gather with Me scatters. I will forgive man speaking against man, but now you go too far when you blaspheme the Spirit of God! This will not be forgiven. Good comes from good trees and a tree is recognized by its fruit. Because of the evil in your hearts, how can anything you say be right? You will be judged for every careless word you speak!"

This exchange is becoming increasingly significant in the hour in which we live. Whole movements within the church, and many individuals in particular, may be in danger of finding themselves in the very place of the Pharisees. Many of the controversies that rock the body of Christ are commonly rooted in suspicion, offense, or accusation, of brother against brother. These controversies turn into a "gang beating" of the character, ministry, history, or doctrine of Christ's servants who walk in the power of the Holy Spirit! Most frightening is that this treachery is commonly found among Pentecostal or Charismatic groups who claim to walk in the fullness of the Spirit!

The word blaspheme in this reference in Matthew is translated "injurious speech; speech that pierces or wounds." Jesus earlier warned His disciples, **"But whoever says, 'You fool!' shall be in danger of hell fire" (Matthew 5:22 NKJV).** Jesus said this in the context that, according to the law, death is penalty for murder. He likened physical murder to the act of slander with the tongue!

To sit in judgment and accuse a fellow man can open one's heart to self righteous pride and deception which will lead to greater sin, just like leaven. Jesus said "a little affects the whole" because it hides in the darkness and grows! Speak against men and soon you will feel free to speak against the works of our Holy God. As the Lord said, **"He who does not gather with Me scatters" (Matthew 12:30 NAS).**

Every good soldier knows that in a time of war, conspiring with the enemy to undermine your commanders, or fellow soldiers, is worthy of execution! Jesus prescribes a chilling penalty for the foolishness of injuring the work of the Holy Spirit battle strategies by speaking against Him— "It won't be forgiven." Jesus points out the obvious: good fruit comes from a good tree. We will give an account before God and our words will acquit or condemn us (see Matthew 12:37). Let us be careful how we dispense our judgments!

Many of the anointed servants of the Lord have been called into account by self-appointed "leaf" inspectors, busybodies, and modern Pharisees. Books denying some of the greatest soul winners of this age have been written and consumed by Christians! These volumes split doctrinal hairs and rail against personal expression or peculiarities of men and women anointed of God as though they were to be judged by us for God's sake. The very reverse is more probably true. Their works towards the lost, the poor, widows and orphans, towards inspiring the discouraged to have faith in God, will judge us!

But we judge and disqualify others, not by their fruit, but by their external appearance—their leaves! Seeking to disqualify them, we are disqualifying ourselves! The Captain of Armies is sure to have severe confrontation in mind for everyone who calls himself a soldier yet devotes his energies to causing divisions in His army, stirring up suspicion, accusation, and fear, in His camp!

There is an interesting parallel between Jesus' discourse on blasphemy in Matthew

> *"To sit in judgment and accuse a fellow man can open one's heart to self righteous pride and deception which will lead to greater sin, just like leaven."*

12 and King David's discourse over the death of Saul in I Samuel Chapter 1. Sometimes a man or woman may depart from the Spirit of God as Saul did and refuse to repent. His or her companions will find that the Holy Spirit will give them an opportunity to separate from them for their own sakes. At that point a decision must be made between human loyalty and obeying the Holy Spirit.

Such must have been the case of Jonathan, Saul's son, who was devoted to David and even foresaw the coming of David's kingdom, yet he died fighting for Saul. On the day Jonathan witnessed Saul's jealousy attempt to murder David with the spear (see I Samuel 18:10), Jonathan should have made the break from his father's deception.

God was allowing His own hand of judgment, through the Philistines, to crush Saul for his wickedness. It was not the time to try to defend the apostate king. However, neither was it right for the righteous to "help God" in bringing about Saul's demise. Those who did would incur a similar fate for themselves!

David's own men reminded him of prophesies that seemed to confirm the fact that he should "help" God by taking Saul's life when he had opportunity. **"This is the day the Lord spoke of when he said to you, 'I will give your enemy into your hands for you to deal with as you wish'"** (I Samuel 24:4 NIV). David rejected this logic, but he did creep up on Saul and cut off a corner of his robe. Then his heart smote him for just doing that! **"The Lord forbid that I should do such a thing to my master, the Lord's anointed, or lift my hand against him; for he is the anointed of the Lord"** (I Samuel 24:6 NIV).

So how should we respond when a leader who has been anointed is taken in a snare of the devil? Remember the sons of Noah. One uncovered the father's nakedness and received a curse. Two others covered him and received blessing (see Genesis 9:20-27). Noah may have put himself in jeopardy of humiliation by becoming drunk, but that did not give his sons the right to expose him. Men of God may put themselves in jeopardy of God's judgment, but if we wrongly try to expose them we are likely to bring judgment upon ourselves as well.

This is not to negate the proper procedures for dealing with sin and bringing discipline within the church. However, many of the attempts to bring correction within the church today are not according to those clearly outlined procedures given to us in Scripture. How can we claim to defend biblical integrity when we do it in a way that violates the very Word of God that we are claiming to defend?

The Amalekite who came to David with the news of Saul's death was obviously thinking that he would be rewarded. He had foolishly involved himself with a situation regarding the Lord's anointed that was none of his business. When he admitted to having had a part in the death of Saul, though he had not actually laid a hand to him, David replied, **"How is it you were not afraid to stretch out your hand to destroy the Lord's**

"Many of the attempts to bring correction within the church today are not according to those clearly outlined procedures given to us in Scripture."

anointed?" (II Samuel 1:14 NAS). If he asked this question of an uncircumcised Amalekite, how much more should we ask this of the church who should know better! David immediately had the man executed. How tragically many today are putting themselves in great danger by so casually lifting their hands against the Lord's anointed, even if those anointed have fallen from grace like Saul had.

David had opportunity to slay Saul as Saul was pursuing David to kill him. Even under these circumstances David said, **"Don't destroy him! Who can lay a hand on the Lord's anointed and be guiltless? As surely as the Lord lives, the Lord himself will strike him; either his time will come and he will die, or he will go into battle and perish. But the Lord forbid that I should lay a hand on the Lord's anointed (I Samuel 26:9-11 NIV)."**

I Samuel tells us that "all the valiant men" went into enemy territory, risking their very own lives, to retrieve the dead bodies of Saul and Jonathan. They did this so that their enemies could no longer gloat over them, and so that God's servants, even though they had fallen, could receive an honorable burial. Like Noah's sons who covered their father's nakedness, they received a blessing.

At news of Saul's death, David took up a lament with weeping and fasting—for a man who had fallen from grace and had even persecuted and tried to kill him! That is the kind of respect that David had for the anointing. David also understood what effect Saul's death would have on Israel and her armies. He knew this tragedy would cause Israel to turn back from her enemies in fear and confusion. This is what Jesus meant when he said, "He who gathers not with Me, scatters."

When David heard the news of Saul's death he said, **"Tell it not in Gath, proclaim it not in the streets of Askelon; lest the daughters of the Philistines rejoice" (II Samuel 1:20 NAS).** How is it that we scour the earth for dirt to publish against other leaders of the body of Christ? Do we esteem some humanistic philosophy of journalism that "the people have a right to know" above the wisdom of the Scriptures? The Amalekite may have had a "good motive" for letting his sword be used to kill Saul, but he was tragically mistaken. The Lord may use the Philistines, the secular media or other means, to bring about His purposes, but woe to us if we wrongfully take such a matter into our own hands.

There is sound military logic in David's command that the fall of Saul not be published. The church has too long considered itself merely some religious political-social organization with an agenda of her own! Not so! We are in the greatest battle of all time against the supreme forces of darkness. We are fighting for the eternal souls of men, women, and children. The nations to whom we have been commissioned to proclaim the gospel may hang in the balance on our carnality! Our actions and our words carry consequences that are more serious than we have acknowledged! For them we will be judged.

David's sentiments surely declare those of our Captain of Hosts as it is said that Jesus sits on the "throne of David." In his

> *"The church has too long considered itself merely some religious political-social organization with an agenda of her own!"*

lament recorded in II Samuel, David curses the very ground where Saul fell. For there, he says, **"the shield of the mighty was defiled, the shield of Saul—no longer rubbed with oil" (II Samuel 1:21 NIV).** David says of this man who continually tried to murder him, **"in life they were loved and gracious" (verse 23).** He was surely calling to mind a perspective far wider than his own persecution and offense regarding Saul! He reminds Israel that Saul's kingship brought them riches and blessing they would not have otherwise enjoyed and they should weep for his death. He remembers Saul as he was in battle against the enemies of Israel, not as he was in his rage against David! He lamented, **"how the mighty have fallen" (verse 27).**

For the sake of our King and His kingdom, it befits us as soldiers to consider those anointed of the Lord as David did. And though we may think we have a right to return evil for an evil done against us, or to take an opportunity to harm an offender, let us choose humility and the fear of God. We must declare with David, "The Lord forbid that I should lay a hand on the Lord's anointed." May we now become like David, a man after God's own heart, and do our best to honor the anointing and the anointed, whether they be Sauls or precious Jonathans. May they always be to us as they were to David, **"swifter than eagles,** and **stronger than lions!" (verse 23).** ■

Bonnie Chavda grew up on a ranch in New Mexico. At the age of 10, a dramatic encounter with the Holy Spirit caused Bonnie to commit her life to Christ and His purposes. The wife of international evangelist, Mahesh Chavda, and mother of four children, Bonnie serves as Executive Director of Mahesh Chavda Ministries International. An inspirational writer and speaker, Bonnie's presentation focuses on personal revival and visitation from the Lord. The Chavdas reside in Charlotte, North Carolina.

✣ Mustard Seeds of Wisdom

"Set yourself always in the lowest place and the highest shall be given you; for the highest cannot stand without the lowest. The chiefest saints before God are the least before themselves, and the more glorious they are, so much within themselves are they more humble."

"Those who are full of truth and heavenly glory are not greedy of vain glory. Those who are firmly settled and grounded in God can no wise be puffed up. And they who ascribe all unto God, whatever good they have received, seek not glory one of another, but wish for that glory which is from God alone and desire above all things that God may be praised in them, and in all His saints; and after this very thing they are always striving."

— *Thomas à Kempis*

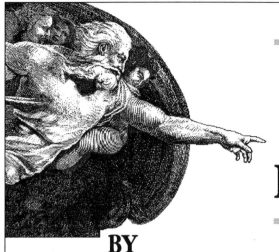

JEALOUSY, OUR HIDDEN SIN

BY JOHN DAWSON

All Scriptures NAS unless otherwise noted.

Do you have jealousy in your heart? How much of your motivation comes from this apparently fickle feeling? "Not much" you might say, but do you really understand the devastating power and subtlety of this inner passion?

You will be surprised at God's perspective on this subject. In our daily lives jealousy towards God is simply evidenced by our refusal to give Him credit for what He alone has done. We withhold from Him that acknowledgement of His worthiness. Thanksgiving and praise are stifled by jealousy and envy.

A Handful of Nothing

Jealousy is a universal motive of the human heart in all work and skill development unless the life of Jesus is being lived through us on a daily basis. We find this sweeping statement in Ecclesiastes 4:4, 6: **"Then I saw that all toil and all skill in work come from a man's envy of his neighbor. This also is vanity and a striving after wind. Better is a handful of quietness than two hands full of toil and a striving after wind"** (RSV). Jealousy is ruthless and uncaring. It is a common motive for murder and cruelty and lays at the root of the actions of a mass murderer like Hitler. **"Wrath is fierce and anger is a flood, but who can stand before jealousy?"** (Proverbs 27:4). **"Jealousy is cruel as the grave: the coals thereof are coals of fire, which hath a most vehement flame"** (Song of Solomon 8:6 KJV).

Jealousy is *hidden* at the root of other motives, influencing our thoughts and actions. As new Christians we quickly deal with areas of obvious sin, but jealousy can lurk in the heart of even a spiritual leader as the deepest motive for seemingly noble conduct. Jeremiah 17:9 states, **"The heart is deceitful above all things, and desperately wicked,"** and poses the question **"Who can know it?"** Only the Spirit of God can discern for us the root of our own motivation. How desperately we need Jesus!

Motive for the First Murder

Let's look at the painful story of the first two little boys who grew up, Cain and Abel.

So it came about in the course of time that Cain brought an offering to the Lord of the fruit of the ground.

And Abel, on his part also brought of the firstlings of his flock and of their fat portions. And the Lord had regard for Abel and for his offering;

but for Cain and for his offering He had no regard. So Cain became very angry and his countenance fell.

Then the Lord said to Cain, "Why are you angry? And why has your countenance fallen?

If you do well, will not your countenance be lifted up? And if you do not do well, sin is crouching at the door; and its desire is for you, but you must master it."

And Cain told Abel his brother. And it came about when they were in the field, that Cain rose up against Abel his brother and killed him (Genesis 4:3-8).

Have you ever really grasped the startling ruthlessness we are capable of when this sin is entertained in our hearts? These brothers lived in a comparatively sin free world as part of the first family. Do you think they had affection for each other? Of course they did, but one murdered the other because of jealousy.

Men are frequently tempted by the lust for honor and recognition. Abel was honored by an authority, Cain was not: **"And the Lord had regard for Abel and for his offering"** (verse 4). A loving heavenly Father counseled with Cain in the midst of his vexation, but he still chose to destroy his brother to satisfy the passion of his jealous soul. The Hebrew word for jealousy is *QIN'A*, meaning deep emotional desire. Never underestimate the power of this sin if unrestrained in your own heart. You may not stoop to murder, but are you a character assassin, destroying the good name of another by innuendo or accusation? Give credit where credit is due.

Envy Is the Enemy of Honesty

The story of Joseph and his brothers in Genesis 37:1-11 is another example of jealousy cruelly tearing brothers apart. **"And his brothers were jealous of him, but his father kept the saying in mind."** After Joseph had declared his dream, his father took him seriously and regarded him as a young man of importance and destiny. This was the last straw for his brothers who conspired to murder him even though he was the youngest.

Then there is the astounding story of David the shepherd boy and Saul the king recorded in I Samuel 18. Saul began by loving David, but was angered by an underling being honored with a greater reputation. **"Then Saul became very angry, for this saying displeased him; and he said, 'They have ascribed to David ten thousands, but to me they have ascribed thousands. Now what more can he have but the kingdom?'"** (I Samuel 18:8).

Jealousy among Men

Men are more vulnerable to jealousy than women in certain areas, particularly in their desire for *power*, *position*, and *title*. We compare ourselves instinctively without thinking about it. Everywhere we look, everything we see—we compare ourselves:

our status, our possessions, our reputation, our relative positioning to that person, to that institution, that object.

We live in a performance-oriented world where we are taught to compete. A man's desire for possessions often has more to do with the prestige he hopes to gain than either the love of an object or the desire for security. All of us need loving appreciation, but to collect envy from the eyes of those whom we have outperformed is a hollow victory indeed. There is no real respect for such a winner—only alienation and loneliness.

Jealousy among Women

The story of Rachel and Leah in Genesis 30 reveals to us some of the particular temptations that affect women. Two sisters are miserably locked into a contest for *acceptance* and *security*—as well as the object possessed by the other, whether it be a child or a handful of flowers.

Terrible roots of insecurity are revealed in Leah's statement, **"Happy am I! For women will call me happy."** and Rachel's **"With mighty wrestlings I have wrestled with my sister."** A summary of this passage would lead us to conclude that a jealous woman must possess the object of another, must gain security through performance, and must gain the acceptance of an authority.

Another obvious vulnerability among women is the status associated with health and beauty. Women are cruelly expected to conform to the images of female beauty present in each culture.

Comparing Ourselves

Let's examine two more biblical examples that reveal the devices of the human heart:

1. *Envy when comparing ourselves with leaders.* The children of Israel envied Moses and Aaron:

> **They quickly forgot His works; they did not wait for His counsel,**
>
> **but craved intensely in the wilderness, and tempted God in the desert.**
>
> **So He gave them their request, but sent a wasting disease among them.**
>
> **When they became envious of Moses in the camp, and of Aaron, the holy one of the Lord,**
>
> **the earth opened and swallowed up Dathan, and engulfed company of Abiram. (Psalm 106:13-17).**

We are so quick to resent the privileges given to those in leadership, but we fail to see the price that has been paid in many years of apprenticeship under God. Moses began to pay that price as a newborn baby. He was set in a basket and floated down the Nile. Those who raged against him did not begin their lives in such danger, and a just God, Who measures all things, judged them harshly.

2. *Envy when comparing ourselves with new or unlikely people God is using.* Do you know why the religious leaders murdered Jesus? Pontius Pilate had a hunch concerning their motivation, so he offered them Barabbas to find out. Barabbas stood for everything they had previously condemned. Jesus stood for everything they were supposed to uphold. **"When therefore they were gathered together, Pilate said to them, 'Whom do you want me to release for you? Barabbas, or Jesus who is called Christ?' For he knew that because of envy they had delivered Him up'"** (Matthew 27:17, 18).

Well, how do you feel? These are the temptations common to us all. Look up to your heavenly Father in simple prayer and ask for His mercy and forgiveness.

There are also terrible consequences for those who continue in this sin. The curse that you have prepared for another will come upon you, and the blessing that you have prepared for yourself will be given to them.

Remember the story of Haman and Mordecai in the book of Esther? Haman was the first Hitler. He committed himself to murder a whole race just because he was not sufficiently honored by one Jew. But what happened? His honors went to Mordecai and his own family was destroyed. He lost his life on the gallows prepared for his enemy. Ezekiel 35:11 is a reference to similar judgment: " 'Therefore, as I live,' declares the Lord God, 'I will deal with you according to your anger and according to your envy which you showed because of your hatred against them' " .

How do we deal with jealousy in our own hearts? First we must see the roots of these thoughts and feelings.

The Roots of Jealousy

1. *A distorted picture of self.* Do you know how really beautiful and valuable you are to Jesus? We live in a performance-oriented world that presses us into its mold of conformity. We must compete with others through our position, appearance, and possessions, or we face rejection. Like salmon leaping at the waterfalls of opportunity, we struggle to dominate others lest we amount to nothing.

Jesus' Kingdom is not like that. The basis of your value and your beauty is really your uniqueness. You were "fearfully and wonderfully made" and never need to envy another. You are an original creation. There has never been a person like you before and there never will be again. Rejoice in your uniqueness, secure in God's love. Only you can fulfill your particular destiny and ministry. We all need *you*.

2. *An inflated picture of self, which is pride.* James 3:14 says, **"But if you have bitter jealousy and selfish ambition in your heart, do not be arrogant and so lie against the truth."** Humility is to see ourselves as we really are. We don't even deserve to live. Your next breath should be drawn with gratitude to God for His mercy. Jealousy is often rooted in self-righteousness. Let us go back to the cross and **"humble ourselves under the mighty hand of God"** (I Peter 5:6).

3. *A twisted picture of God in His justice.* Is God always just? Of course He is. Then why are we bent out of shape when somebody else receives blessing? We are failing to see the mercy of God in our own lives and failing to admit our own partiality. Trust your heavenly Father. He does what's best for you.

4. *Fear and insecurity in your relationship with God.* Why do we become depressed when that other woman has a new baby or that other family moves into a beautiful new home? Why are spiritual leaders encouraged, yet also strangely discouraged, when they hear reports of a great victory in another person's ministry? It stems from the subconscious belief that the blessing of others is a sign of God's greater love for them. Psalm 49:16 says, **"Do not be afraid when a man becomes rich, when the glory of his house is increased."**

Each of these four roots is in some way a distortion of the truth about ourselves or about God. We must honestly face up to our need and ask God for a further revelation of His loving heart.

continued on page 85

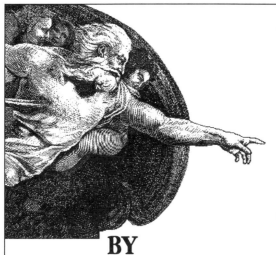

CATCHING THE NEXT WAVE

BY RICK JOYNER

All Scriptures NAS unless otherwise noted.

There is a great spiritual advance that is now gaining momentum throughout the body of Christ. It has the potential to be as sweeping in its scope and impact as the greatest movements of church history. How can we discern it accurately, and position ourselves properly to be a part of it?

Moves of the Holy Spirit are often compared to waves because their characteristics are common. If the Holy Spirit moves in waves, how do we catch them so as to be carried in the direction that He is going? There are four basic steps that a surfer uses that can give us significant insight into what we too must do to catch the waves of the Holy Spirit. If a surfer is going to catch a wave he must first discern where it is going to break. Second, he must position himself properly at that point. Third, he must begin to move in the direction that the wave is going. Then he must not hesitate when it breaks, or it will just pass him by.

Looking Back to Look Ahead

Many are discerning enough to know that the Holy Spirit is moving again, but are doing very little to position themselves properly to be a part of it. Every move of God is built upon the foundation of the previous moves. If we are going to discern where the next move of God is going to break, we need to discern the nature and pattern of the previous ones.

There is a spiritual "continuation principle" that we must understand, and submit to, if we are going to be a part of a move of the Holy Spirit. That is why Jesus submitted Himself to John's baptism. To "fulfill all righteousness" even the Lord had to properly honor those who had gone before Him and prepared His way. When Jesus was asked by the chief priests and elders:

"By what authority are You doing these things, and who gave You this authority?"

He replied: "I will ask you one thing too, which if you tell Me, I will also tell you by what authority I do these things.

The baptism of John was from what source, from heaven or from men?" (Matthew 21:23-25).

The Lord's response to their question was not an attempt to deflect their question—the answer to His question was the answer to their question. Jesus had credentials. John was there as the representative of the "old order," sent to declare that Jesus was in fact the one that all of the prophets and wise men from the beginning had been speaking of.

Honor with Righteous Judgment

If we arrogantly point to previous movements as "the old order," and declare ourselves to be of "the new order," we have almost certainly disqualified ourselves from being a part of the new order. It will be those who view the previous movements with the honor they deserve, who will immerse themselves in their message and teachings, who will be qualified to receive the next level of authority. For any new movement to abide long on the earth it must honor its spiritual fathers and mothers.

James gave an interesting exhortation concerning treatment of the Law, which was the "movement" that preceded Christianity:

Do not speak against one another, brethren. He who speaks against a brother, or judges his brother, speaks against the law, and judges the law; but if you judge the law, you are not a doer of the law, but a judge of it.

There is only one Lawgiver and Judge, the One who is able to save and to destroy; but who are you who judge your neighbor?

Do not complain, brethren, against one another, that you yourselves may not be judged; behold, the Judge is standing right at the door (James 4:11, 12; 5:9).

When we judge in such a way that we are criticizing, we are condemning ourselves to the opposition of God, Who **"resists the proud, but gives grace to the humble" (James 4:6 NKJV).** Criticism is one of the highest forms of pride. When we criticize others we are by that declaring ourselves to be superior to them. This may be true, but if we are better than others it is only because of God's grace. To become proud of our own standing is to depart from the very foundation upon which we are standing—God's grace.

However, there is a "righteous judgment" that we must have. We are foolish if we do not try to learn from the mistakes of the previous movements. Even so, we must be careful how we view them, not as condemning our spiritual parents, but seeing where the potential for the same faults exists within us so that we can seek the grace to stand in those areas.

The failure to properly understand righteous and unrighteous judgment is the reason for many of the greatest failures of the church in history, and is one of the most important issues facing the church today. Until we understand them, and walk by that understanding, we will continue to stumble over a deadly stumbling block.

The church both historically and presently has been prone to use unrighteous judgment while utterly neglecting the righteous judgment. Many watchdog ministries and Christian journalists have stumbled while sincerely trying to help fill a tragic void in church government. They fall because they have moved into a realm of authority to which they have not been appointed. Meanwhile, the elders neglect the authority which they have been given to exercise. Every new movement will continue to fall short of its potential until this important issue is resolved.

Paddling with the Wave

Some are both discerning where the next wave is going to break, and are positioning themselves properly, but are hesitant about moving until the wave is upon them. These are in as much danger of missing the wave as those who have not positioned themselves at all. The most important thing that we can do to be moving with the wave when it comes is to obey and implement that which was imparted to the church through the last move.

A major source of the hesitancy that causes many to miss the moves of the Holy Spirit is a religious spirit rooted in human idealism that will not move until something is "totally God." The Lord does not do anything without man. A farmer was once being congratulated by a minister on the precision and lushness of his cornfield, remarking that he could not have done that without God. "I agree," said the farmer, "But He could not do it without me either. You should see the field I let Him grow by Himself. It's all weeds!"

There is an important point to this story. God commissioned man to "cultivate the garden." Man's work on earth is not unnatural, but man is a part of the nature of the world which God created. Likewise, He has commissioned fallible men to do the work of the ministry. Even the greatest man of God is an earthen vessel, imperfect and frail. As James explained, **"We all stumble in many ways"** (James 3:2).

The Lord left the church in the hands of men who appeared to be quite unstable and prone to mistakes, and they did make mistakes. We all must grow in grace and wisdom. If we had to wait until we were perfect to minister, no one would ever be qualified. Perfectionists who require unrealistic standards are like the Pharisees who would not enter the kingdom themselves, and tried to hinder everyone else from entering as well. Every true move of God has begun with a considerable amount of humanity mixed in at first. There will always be tares mixed in with the wheat. If you are going to wait until all of the tares are removed you will miss the entire harvest.

Wait for the Big One

There is another factor that is required if we want to catch the biggest wave—we must resist catching the smaller ones. There are patterns to incoming waves which experienced surfers learn to recognize. Patience is required if they are going to ride the biggest and best wave. Likewise, in the Spirit there are many movements to which we can give ourselves, and many projects we can become involved in, but are they what we have been called to? How many of these are only working to displace us from our position when the big one comes?

This is not to discourage anyone from devotion to service and ministry. Indeed, the only way that we will be in shape and skilled enough to catch the big wave is by practicing on the smaller ones. However, when we have been adequately prepared, and we know that the big one is coming, we must let the smaller ones go by. Many who miss the great moves of God do so because they are already too busy.

The Opposition

Each wave will try to make it as far up the beach as it can. Then the wave recedes, undercutting the next wave, making it break sooner than it would otherwise. Seldom have those who were a part of one move of God gone on to be a part of the next move. Usually those of a previous move are retreating as the next wave advances, creating a clash that hinders the next incoming wave. For every incoming wave, some of its greatest opposition will be from the previous waves that are retreating.

Throughout church history those who were a part of one move of God have tried to resist and undercut those of the next move. However, even though this has continually been our history, it does not have to be our future. Before the end there will be a movement that will capture the hearts of those in the previous movements so that they will join the advance rather than continue the retreat. When this happens the church will begin a spiritual advance that will not be stopped until the end of the age.

Looking at some of the historic factors that have caused others to retreat can help us discern these stumbling blocks. The first dangerous delusion is for us to think that we would never oppose a true move of God. It has happened to some of the greatest men of God in history. The arrogance that it cannot happen to us can be the very thing that disqualifies us from God's grace, which He only gives to the humble (see James 4:6).

Andrew Murray is a good example of how even a great man of God, with a passion for seeing revival come to the church, can fail to recognize the very revival that he had spent his entire life praying for. The cause for this tragic failure was simple. The revival that he hoped for, and even prophesied, did not come in the form that he was expecting. Though he earnestly desired to see the release of spiritual gifts within the church again, he was offended by the package they arrived in.

Unfortunately, most new movements are led by relatively immature leaders. This is because the mature leaders have become "old wineskins," too inflexible to receive the new wine. Spiritual movements must be led by the Spirit, Who requires flexibility and openness. Usually the only ones He can find that are flexible enough are the immature, because they have not yet become inflexible with preconceived ideas. Immature leaders are therefore more prone to be dependent on the Holy Spirit than on their experience, allowing Him to direct as He chooses. This is probably why the Lord chose such unlikely and "unqualified" men as the foundational leaders of His church. They were so unqualified that they were desperately dependent upon His grace and guidance.

True Faith

Rarely does there arise a spiritual leader with great experience and wisdom, combined with a sensitive dependency upon the Holy Spirit. However, such leadership is certainly preferable to that of the immature. The immature do allow the Holy Spirit to lead, which is the highest form of wisdom, but they often allow other influences to gain entry because of their lack of experience. It is for this reason that the Lord always seems to give opportunity to leaders of previous movements to lead the next move. The greatest leaders will know how to let the Holy Spirit lead, while having the experience and discernment to keep the movement out of the hands of the lawless or legalistic.

Two good biblical examples of those with maturity and experience combined with flexibility and dependency on the Holy Spirit are Joshua and Caleb. Such will also be required for the movement that leads the church across her Jordan River into the battle for her Promised Land. Not only were Joshua and Caleb men of great faith in the Lord, but their faith was not diluted by many years of wandering in the wilderness with a faithless people.

Such faith could only be the result of two great spiritual factors. First, true faith is not encouraged or discouraged by the condition of the people, because it is not faith in people but in God. Second, true faith is not limited by time but always views from the perspective of eternity. That is why the great men of faith in Scripture were content to view the fulfillment of the promises prophetically without having to receive them in their own time.

It is most difficult to grow in wisdom, experience and age compared to other men while remaining humble. This is because of our tendency to judge ourselves by our comparison to other men, rather than to the only true Standard—Christ Jesus. Measuring ourselves by other men, or our church by other churches, is one of the most deadly stumbling blocks to spiritual leaders. As Paul said, "… **but when they measure themselves by themselves, and compare themselves with themselves,** **they are without understanding" (II Corinthians 10:12b).**

" One of the greatest stumbling blocks to walking in true ministry is the tendency to take the people's yokes instead of the Lord's yoke. The people's yokes will have us busy doing many things that appear good and fruitful, but they will not have us doing the Lord's will. "

True faith does not look at men and it does not look at the temporary. Some of the Lord's most anointed messages caused the crowds to shrink. The truly wise will not be overly encouraged when men gather around them, or discouraged when they depart. If we receive our encouragement from men it only proves that we have received our authority from men. If we receive our authority from above then no man can take it away, and we will not be overly concerned by either the approval or disapproval of men. That is why when men came to make Jesus king He fled to the mountains. If men make you king then men will also rule you, regardless of what title you are given.

Jesus unquestionably had the greatest compassion for the human condition. However, He never responded to human need—He only did what He saw the Father doing. The Lord did not just call us to do good works in His name, but to do the work that He called us to do. One of the greatest stumbling blocks to walking in true ministry is the tendency to take the people's yokes instead of the Lord's yoke. The people's yokes will have us busy doing many things that appear good and fruitful, but they will not have us doing the Lord's will.

How many of us could, like Philip, begin a revival that stirs an entire city, then give that work into the hands of others so that we can go witness to just one man? The reason that Philip could be entrusted with such authority and power to stir a city was because of his obedience. If he were just focused on men, or the temporary, he would never have left Samaria. However, it is probable that the fruit of that one Ethiopian eunuch's conversion was much greater than the revival in Samaria. Centuries later missionaries were astonished to find that when they arrived in Ethiopia there were so many Christians already there. This fruit had been hidden to men, and probably even to Philip, but it was certainly credited to his account.

Obedience, Not Sacrifice

It is obedience, not sacrifice, that will keep us in the will of God. I do not think that I have ever met a true Christian that did not long to be in the center of the activity of God. However, we must know that not all good activity is God's activity. We must also understand that it is not possible for all of us to be a part of everything that He is doing. The most important issue is not just catching the "big wave," but catching the one that He wants us to catch, while cheering on those who may be catching the bigger ones, and the smaller ones, if they are in God's will.

As we keep our vision on the goal of seeing the water move as far up the beach as possible, and holding all of the ground that we can take, we will be in a better position to move forward with the next wave rather than retreating and undercutting it. It does not matter who leads a wave as long as The Leader gets the glory. To have any other attitude is to be as deluded as the donkey's colt that Jesus rode into Jerusalem on, if he thought that all of the commotion and adoration was for him instead of the One riding on his back.

Jan Amos Comenius stated that "Nature is God's second book." The apostle Paul affirmed this in the first chapter of Romans. One of the great leadership lessons in nature is found with migrating waterfowl such as geese and ducks. They fly in "V" formations because the lead bird creates a draft that makes the flying easier for those who follow closely behind him. However, since the lead bird cutting through the air is doing the most work, he will only stay on the point for a period of time, and then he will drop back to the end of the formation and rest. This rotation allows the birds to share the burden of leadership, and all benefit from the draft when others are leading. If a bird refused to give up his leadership position at the proper time he would begin to slow down the whole flock. Those who give up their position at the proper time will have a chance to rest while following in the wake of others, enabling them to again assume the point at another time.

Seldom in church history has any leader been on the cutting edge for more than a few years. However, it is a most difficult thing for a leader to give up leadership. For those who refused to do this there is a clear demarcation point in their lives when they stopped going forward and started attacking those who did.

Flying geese do not have as their goal being the point bird, but rather getting to the destination. Whenever our own position becomes a goal in itself we will become more of a hindrance to the advancement of the church than a leader of it. One can have great influence and control other people long after he has lost the true anointing for spiritual leadership.

King Saul is one of the more obvious biblical examples of this principle.

Saul's counterpart, King David, was not just an extraordinary leader in his own time, but he had the wisdom to realize the limits of his authority. When he understood that it was not his destiny to build the temple, he began gathering materials to pass on to his heir in order to make his job easier. The greatest leaders not only know how far to go themselves—they know how to prepare for the next generation, and when to pass the scepter.

Summary

Leadership is a valuable gift. The desire to be on the cutting edge of what God is doing, to be in the middle of the action, is usually evidence of our love for the Lord and our desire to a part of what He is doing. However, if our motives are not right, it can also be one of our most prideful, and disobedient pursuits. It is right to want to push back the darkness, to help the body of Christ climb to higher ground, but are we doing this for the Lord's glory or for our own? If we are not doing it for ourselves we should be just as glad to prepare for others to do it, and to cheer them on. Is

that not what the great cloud of witnesses is doing right now for us?

Being on the cutting edge, or being with a group that is, is not the most important goal in life. When we stand before the throne of God on that great judgment day, He is not going to count how many cutting edge movements we were a part of. We are going to be judged by our obedience, and by how much of His likeness we bear. In Christ it is true that the greatest leaders are the greatest followers. The more closely we follow Him, the more of His glory we will behold, and the more like Him we will become.

To fulfill all righteousness, and to walk in the spiritual authority to which we have been called, requires that we properly honor those who have gone before us and have made our way easier. It is also true that we must be willing to prepare the way for those who will carry the work further. We must all be willing to let go, when the time is right. It was David's willingness to pass on to the next generation what was the greatest desire of his own heart that enabled God to entrust him with the extraordinary leadership for his own generation. ■

✜ Mustard Seeds of Wisdom

"Every word of Christ, every act, was simple, sincere, and dignified. The entire New Testament breathes the same spirit.... It is significant that the two greatest movements within the church since Pentecost, the sixteenth century Reformation and the Wesley revival, were characterized by sobriety and sincerity. They both reached the roots of society and touched the masses; yet they never descended to be common or to pander to carnal flesh. The quality of their preaching was lofty, serious, and dignified, and their singing the same."

— A. W. Tozer

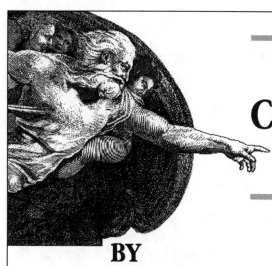

GOD'S CHAMPIONSHIP TEAM

BY
REGGIE WHITE

All Scriptures NAS unless otherwise noted.

Can you imagine what a football team would be like if no one was accountable to anyone else? The coach sends a play in during a game, and the quarterback doesn't like it so he changes it. The running backs don't want to follow the quarterback's call, so they decide to just stand still and watch. The receivers don't like either the quarterback's call or the running backs' decision, so they go get some Gatorade on the sidelines. It sounds ridiculous. Such a team would be in chaos, with no hope of ever winning. But how many churches are just like that? There must be someone in leadership.

The very same principle applies to a person's spiritual life. We all must be accountable to someone greater than ourselves. Christians have chosen Jesus Christ to be the coach of our lives. Do we follow His instructions? Are we accountable to the rest of His team? Just as a football player must be accountable and in harmony with the team on every play, we must be in harmony with God's team every day.

The Bible is God's playbook. It contains everything we need to live the most abundant life possible on this earth. Everyone in the church needs to know the Bible just as everyone on the team needs to know the same playbook. If we don't follow the same plays at the same time there will be chaos. That chaos is in the church is just as apparent to the world as it is if you watch a game on T.V. and the players go the wrong way. If each person does not do his assignment properly, with all of his heart, the team will not succeed.

On a football team players are first accountable to the coach. Since the coach can't be on the field during the game, he appoints key players on the field to make sure his plans get carried out. On offense it's usually the quarterback that gives the instructions from the coach. On defense one of the linebackers gives the assignment on each play. Players know that during the game they must give the coach's designated captain the same attention that they would give the coach.

Christians are accountable to Jesus Christ and His commands. We are just as accountable when they come through His "captains" as we are when they come directly from Him. Anything less is what the Bible calls lawlessness and it will create confusion and defeat. As John explained:

This is how we know that we love the children of God: by loving God and carrying out his commands. This is love for God: to obey his commands. And his commands are not burdensome (I John 5:2, 3).

Accountability does not stop with the quarterback and linebackers. Each player is responsible to his teammates for making the play successful. If one player anticipates something from the opposition he is supposed to alert the others. For example, a linebacker may notice that the opposing team's alignment signifies that the play is going to the left. He may not have time to go to the coach and confirm this, so he will go straight to the captain, or to the other players who will be most affected. Everyone is responsible to be discerning, and possibly to give some direction, but this is always done in harmony with the team, not out of self-will. This is the result of everyone pulling together, not going their own way.

If someone's discernment is consistently wrong, he will lose authority on the team. The other players will not be as responsive to his insights. Authority is based on faithfulness, having a record of dependability, accuracy, and having the team's best interest in mind. When you hear about players having "leadership," that is what they are talking about. They are good representatives of the coach on the field. The same is true of spiritual leadership. The greatest leaders will be those who best represent the Lord in the world.

The Home Team

Every church needs to be a team. The better the team learns to work together the more successful it will be. The same is true with our families. Second only to the Lord, I'm accountable to my wife, Sara. I know I can depend on her to tell it like it is. God always uses Sara to affirm or negate whatever may surface in my life. We are a team. We are playing for each other and not against each other. She has my best interests in mind and I have hers. We are competing together against the spirit of this world. One of the enemy's main strategies to defeat us is to get us competing with each other.

"One of the enemy's main strategies to defeat us is to get us competing with each other."

I'm also accountable to some Christian friends who give me sound spiritual guidance. I know they will shoot straight with me from their own experiences, as well as from God's Word. Any one of them can talk to me for just a few minutes and discern whether I'm walking close to the Lord or if I might just need a spiritual kick in the seat of my pants. I can really count on them to tell me when I'm straying off the path—whether I ask them to do so or not. We all have blind spots, areas in our lives which hinder our spiritual growth, but areas that we cannot see. If we don't watch out for each other we will take many unnecessary shots from the enemy.

If we are not accountable to someone it will be very hard for others to accept our leadership. A linebacker who is prone to doing his own thing will never be trusted as a captain on the team. We must learn to accept constructive criticism ourselves if we expect others to accept our correction. As the proverb declares: **"Stern discipline awaits him who leaves the path; he who hates correction will die" (Proverbs 15:10).**

Some Christians don't feel comfortable pointing out other Christians' errors. It's true that we usually shouldn't be going around advising others of their shortcomings, unless they ask us to. However, there are exceptions to this, such as when another Christian sins against us. The Lord directed us how to respond to this:

> **If your brother sins against you, go and show him his fault, just between the two of you. If he listens to you, you have won your brother over.**
>
> **But if he will not listen, take one or two others along, so that "every matter may be established by the testimony of two or three witnesses."**
>
> **If he refuses to listen to them, tell it to the church; and if he refuses to listen even to the church, treat him as you would a pagan or a tax collector. (Matthew 18:15-17)**

This command is given to keep us from doing one of the primary things that can break down the spirit of a team—gossip. Often when someone sins against us we want to tell others about it, but that is gossip. Gossip does not just involve telling lies about someone. A good definition of gossip is: expressing your opinion about a matter when you are neither a part of the problem nor the solution. Ephesians 4:29 commands us to: **"Let no unwholesome word proceed from your mouth, but only such a word as is good for edification according to the need of the moment, that it may give grace to those who hear."**

An opposing football team is always looking for the weakness of their opponent so they can exploit it and defeat them. Our enemy is always looking for a weakness in our team, both in the church and in our families. Our spiritual weakness can always be defined by sin. Whenever he sees a sin he will run his play right for that point. If he sees a Christian sin against another Christian he has spotted a major weakness which he knows can begin the unraveling of the whole team. That's why if a brother sins against us we do need to go and get it straight with him just as soon as we can to keep the enemy from exploiting it. This must always be done in such a way as to help our teammates, and therefore the whole team.

The Necessity for Accountability

On a football team, when a player continues to gripe about mistakes and hurts the team, he must be told. However, we must go to him, not to the other teammates. If we don't go to him, we are hurting the team as much as he is. Everyone makes mistakes, and the truly wise players appreciate having others tell them what they are doing wrong so they can correct it. As Solomon put it: **"He is on the path of life who heeds instruction, but he who forsakes reproof goes astray" (Proverbs 10:17).**

However, when we correct each other we must be sure that we do it in the right spirit or it can do more damage than good. Proverbs 12:18 says, **"There is one who speaks rashly like the thrusts of a sword, but the tongue of the wise brings healing."** Our correction should always be for the purpose of helping our teammates, not just because we are irritated. There is no telling how many sins committed by Christians could have been averted if someone had gone to them with Godly correction instead of just criticizing them.

The Spiritual Hospital

My pastor in Tennessee, Rev. Jerry Upton, had an incredible vision about the damage we bring upon ourselves. In the vision he was taken to a large hospital where he was given a tour conducted by the Lord. The hospital had three wards filled with many hurting Christians.

The first ward contained about a hundred believers who were discouraged and depressed because they had never gotten off the ground in their faith. The Lord told him not to worry about these people because they were cared for by several doctors and nurses, who were actually ministers and other mature believers. These spiritual doctors and nurses edified and built up the suffering Christians with real discernment and encouragement. These believers would be restored to good spiritual health because they were involved with other more mature Christians.

Then the Lord took my pastor to the second ward. Here people had been hurt more deeply than those in the first ward. He was told that these Christians had gone forth in spiritual warfare against the enemy and had been injured; they needed repair and nurturing back to sound spiritual health. Fewer doctors and nurses were around, but the Lord assured him that these

> *"When one team member is hurt, the whole team is weakened. We must stop criticizing and tearing each other down, and begin to build each other up."*

also would return to spiritual wholeness because of the care they would receive.

Before he entered the third ward, the Lord told him to prepare his heart for something he had never witnessed. Even so, he couldn't believe his eyes when he entered that ward. Some people's heads were half blown off; arms were missing from some and legs from others. But the difference between this and the other two wards was blatantly visible: not one doctor and not one nurse ministered to these believers. They just laid there, with no hope for recovery. When my pastor asked the Lord who these people were, the Lord's answer cut him to the very quick of his soul.

The Lord told him, "These believers have been wounded by other believers. There are no doctors or nurses because the first thing a Christian wounded by another Christian does is isolate himself from any form of ministry. Many of these will not make it back to spiritual wholeness."

The Bible tells us that Satan cannot touch a Christian unless God gives him permission, as He did in the case of Job. So, how in the world can Satan get to believers? He accomplishes this by attacking Christians through other Christians. The only way a believer can be devoured by Satan is through another believer! Remember Paul's warning: **"If you keep on biting and devouring each other, watch out or you will be destroyed by each other" (Galatians 5:15).**

All believers in Jesus Christ are on the same team and are accountable to each other. When one team member is hurt, the whole team is weakened. We must stop criticizing and tearing each other down, and begin to build each other up. Yes, we must confront one another when necessary, and we must practice accountability, but we must do all things in a spirit of love. As the Apostle John reminds us: **"All men will know that you are my disciples, if you love one another" (John 13:35).** Every time the world expects us to show anger and bitterness, but we show love, we have scored a touchdown!

The old song goes, "And they will know we are Christians by our love." We must get along with other Christians, regardless of what label they wear. We must stop running down other churches and believers just because their relationship with the Lord is not like ours. I am a defensive player on my team, but I am rooting just as hard for the offense and special teams to succeed.

The common ground for fellowship with other Christians is their belief in and following of Jesus Christ. Not doctrine, not form of worship, not dress, not hair style—a simple belief in and acceptance of Jesus Christ as Lord and Savior is all that is required. Even the disciples struggled with this:

> **"Master," said John, "we saw a man driving out demons in your name and we tried to stop him, because he is not one of us."**
>
> **"Do not stop him," Jesus said, "for whoever is not against you is for you" (Luke 9:49, 50).**

John was upset because the guy was not a part of their group. At another time John had wanted to call fire down on those who rejected the Lord. But John was accountable to Jesus and the Lord was able to correct him. Later John seemed to become the most loving and tolerant of the apostles. We must not keep relating to each other the way we are now, but we must see each other as God has called us to be. Godly correction will change us all; but we must remain in a place where we can receive it.

Until we as the body of Christ get right with each other, we're never going to solve the abortion problem. We're never going to have any effect on the divorce rate as long as churches are splitting. As a matter of fact, we're never going to accomplish anything until we learn to love each other as God commands us to do. The team where members truly love each other will be unbeatable because **"love never fails" (I Corinthians 13:8).**

Our Coach is now putting together such a team, and He has a special place for each of us on it. But we must all learn that we are a team, and none of us will succeed until all of us do. ■

Reggie White is a defensive lineman for the Green Bay Packers. A future Hall of Famer, he is considered by many to be one of the best defensive players of all time. Reggie is also an ordained Baptist minister and the founder of The National Society of Nehemiah, which is devoted to inner-city ministry. The following is a modified article taken from Reggie's book *Minister of Defense*, which can be found in Christian bookstores everywhere, or may be ordered directly from MorningStar Publications.

✣ Mustard Seeds of Wisdom

"I do not pray for a lighter load, but a stronger back."

— *Philip Brooks*

UPROAR IN THE CHURCH

BY DEREK PRINCE

All Scriptures NKJV unless otherwise noted.

Reports have been coming in from Christian groups in widely separated locations of what appears to be a strange new phenomenon. Believers of different ages and widely different social backgrounds are being overcome by prolonged outbursts of laughter which have no obvious cause. Sometimes they may also act as if they are drunk.

Often this laughter appears to be contagious. Those who have experienced it apparently "transmit" it to others. Large groups may be seized by it simultaneously.

Both ministers and lay people from a wide range of denominations have been affected in this way. Some testify that it has had a stimulating effect on their faith and has brought them closer to the Lord. On the other hand, there are those who are skeptical and view this kind of experience as a deception of the enemy.

As a result of all this, I am frequently being asked whether I believe that the Holy Spirit at times produces in people prolonged, exuberant and apparently causeless laughter. "I have to believe it," I reply, "because that is how I was saved more than 50 years ago."

In the summer of 1941, I was part of a medical unit of the British Army billeted in a hotel on the North Bay of Scarborough in Yorkshire. The hotel had been gutted of all its furniture and fittings. Our "beds" were simply straw mattresses on the floor.

While in Scarborough I had some brief contacts with Pentecostal Christians, who confronted me for the first time with my need to receive Christ as my personal Savior. At that point in my life I was a nominal Anglican, who never voluntarily attended church. I had never before heard of Pentecostals, and I had no idea what they believed or what kind of people they were.

About nine months previously, however, I had started to read the Bible through from beginning to end. I had no religious motive. I regarded the Bible merely as a work of philosophy. As a professional philosopher, I felt it was my academic duty to find out what the Bible had to say. At this point I had come as far as the book of Job—but it had been a dreary task!

Confronted in this way with the claims of Christ, however, I decided about 11 o'clock one night to pray "until something happened." I had no idea what I might expect to happen. For about an hour I struggled in vain to form some kind of coherent prayer. Then about midnight I became aware of a presence and I found myself saying to some unknown person what Jacob had said when wrestling with the angel at Peniel: **"Unless you bless me, I will not let you go" (Genesis 32:26).**

I repeated these words several times with increasing emphasis: "I will not let you go, I will not let you go…" Then I began to say to the same unknown person, "Make me love you more and more". When I got to these last words, I again began to repeat them; "more and more and more…"

At this point an invisible power came down over me and I found myself on my back on the floor, with my arms in the air, still saying, "more and more and more…."

After a while my words changed to deep sobbing which rose up from my belly through my lips, shaking my whole body convulsively. The sobs did not proceed out of anything in my conscious mind. I had no special sense of being sinful.

After about half an hour, without any act of my volition, the sobbing changed to laughter. I had no more conscious reason for laughing than I had for sobbing. The laughter, like the sobbing, flowed from my belly. At first, it was quite gentle, but it gradually became louder and louder. I had the impression that I was being immersed in a sea of laughter that reverberated around the room.

At this point the soldier who shared the room with me woke up to find me on my back on the floor clothed only in my underwear, with my arms in the air, laughing uproariously. Rising up from his mattress, he walked around me rather helplessly two or three times, keeping at a safe distance. Finally he said, "I don't know what to do with you. I suppose it's no good pouring water over you." An inaudible voice within me responded, "Even water wouldn't put this out!"

However, I remembered dimly having heard years earlier in church that men should not blaspheme the Holy Spirit. Contrary to all my natural reasoning, I knew that what was in me was the Holy Spirit. In order not to offend my friend, I rolled over onto my face and laboriously crawled to my mattress. Pulling the blanket over my head, I eventually fell asleep, still laughing—quietly.

Next morning I awoke to an amazing, but objective, fact: I was a totally different person. No longer did vile language flow out of my mouth. Prayer was no longer an effort, it was as natural as breathing. I could not even drink a glass of water without pausing to thank God for it.

At six o'clock, as was my usual custom, I went to the pub for a drink. But when I got to the door, my legs "locked." They would not carry me inside the pub. I stood there having an argument with my legs. Then, to my surprise, I realized I was no longer interested in what the pub had to offer. I turned round and walked back to my billet.

Back in my billet once again, I opened my Bible to continue reading. At this point, however, I discovered the most amazing change of all. Overnight the Bible had become a completely new book. It was as if there were only two persons in the universe—God and me. The Bible was God speaking directly and personally to me.

This has never changed, and it is equally true of the Old Testament and the New.

I opened by chance at Psalm 126:1, 2: **"When the Lord turned again the captivity of Zion, we were like them that dream. Then our mouth was filled with laughter..." (KJV).**

At that point I paused, "That's exactly what happened to me," I thought. "It wasn't I who was laughing. My mouth was being filled with laughter from some other source!" Upon further reflection, I saw that this strange, supernatural laughter was the way that God's people expressed their joy and excitement at being delivered from captivity.

Turning back to Job I came across another passage that apparently referred to the same strange phenomenon: **"Behold, God will not cast away a perfect man.... Till He fill thy mouth with laughing, and thy lips with shouting for joy" (Job 8:20, 21 KJV Margin)**

In this case, too, I saw that the laughter did not proceed from a person's own will, but actually from God Himself. Furthermore, it was a response to the assurance of "not being cast away"—that is, of God's acceptance.

As I read on into the Psalms, I made a further discovery: God Himself laughs. Furthermore, God's laughter is not—as we in the West think of it—a reaction to something comical. It is the expression of total triumph over His enemies.

When earth's rulers decide to reject God's government, what is God's response? **"He that sitteth in the heavens shall laugh: the Lord shall have them in derision" (Psalm 2:4 KJV).**

Again, when the wicked plots against the righteous, God's reaction is the same:

"The Lord shall laugh at him: for he seeth that his day is coming" (Psalm 37:13 KJV).

Psalm 59 opens with a vivid description of the evil activities of unregenerate men, but once more the Lord responds in the same way: **"But thou, O Lord, shalt laugh at them: thou shalt have all the heathen in derision" (Psalm 59:8 KJV).**

When the righteous see God's inexorable judgment on the wicked, it is natural that they, too, should respond in the same way as God Himself. **"The righteous shall see, and fear, and shall laugh at him" (Psalm 52:6 KJV).**

There was another area, too, in which the Bible shed its light on all that had been happening to me. I came to see the identity of the person I had been asking to bless me. It was Jesus of Nazareth—the same person whom Jacob had encountered at Peniel. Jacob had encountered Him before His incarnation; I had encountered Him after His resurrection.

I could find no other way to explain the related passages of scripture. The person whom Jacob encountered was both a man and God—and also an angel, that is, a messenger from God to man. (See Genesis 32:24-30, Hosea 12:3-4) There is only one person in the universe who answers to that description, the one who came to earth in human form as Jesus of Nazareth.

One evening about ten days after my first encounter with the Lord, I was lying on my back on my mattress in the billet and I began to speak an unfamiliar language that sounded to me like Chinese. Once again, I dimly recalled something I had heard in church about "speaking with other tongues." I knew it was connected somehow with the day of Pentecost. At first I spoke timidly and hesitantly, but as

I relaxed, the flow of words became free and forceful.

Once again, the initiative did not come from me. I was responding to a powerful inner force that came very specifically - like my previous laughter - from my belly.

The following evening I again found myself speaking an unknown language, but it was obviously different from the language I had been speaking the previous evening. This time I noticed that the words had a very marked poetic rhythm.

After a few moments of silence, I began to speak in English, but the words were not of my choosing, and their content was on a level far above that of my own understanding. Also, they seemed to have a rhythm similar to that of the words that I had previously spoken in an unknown language. I concluded that my words in English were an interpretative rendering of what I had previously said in the unknown language.

One brief section of what I said in English remains indelibly impressed upon my memory. In vivid imagery it outlined God's plan for my life. Looking back over more than 50 years, I can see how God's plan has been—and is still being—progressively worked out in my life.

In retrospect, too, I have gained a new understanding of my initial experience of supernatural laughter. Unconventional as it was, it proved to be the divinely appointed door through which I entered a lifelong walk of faith. It also had the effect of liberating me from many preconceptions of my background and culture which could have been a barrier to my further spiritual progress.

In Matthew 12:33 Jesus states the most decisive test that must be applied to all forms of spiritual experience: **"a tree is known by its fruit."** I have to ask myself therefore: What has been the fruit of my strange experience? Is it possible to give an objective answer?

Yes, the fruit of that experience has been a life converted from sin to righteousness, from agnostic dabbling in the occult to unshakable faith in Jesus Christ as He is revealed in the Scriptures—a life that has been bringing forth fruit in God's Kingdom for well over 50 years. Certainly that was no transient product of autosuggestion or of some mere emotional extravagance.

> *"From time to time, in the succeeding years, I have received a renewed experience of supernatural laughter. I have also seen other believers touched by God in a similar way, but this has never been a main emphasis of my teaching."*

From time to time, in the succeeding years, I have received a renewed experience of supernatural laughter. I have also seen other believers touched by God in a similar way, but this has never been a main emphasis of my teaching. Almost invariably I have found that this kind of laughter has a double effect: it is both cleansing and exhilarating. At times it has been accompanied by miracles of physical healing or of deliverance from emotional conditions such as depression.

Exercising Discernment

My own experience of supernatural laughter took place about midnight in an army billet more than 50 years ago. There now appears to be a widespread eruption of similar manifestations among Christian groups in many different locations. A minister friend has told me of uproarious laughter erupting spontaneously in Siberia among Christians who had no contact with the West. Similar reports have come from parts of Europe.

More recently, various other unconventional manifestations have been reported—including some that are positively bizarre. In Britain, this new move apparently started in London, then spread to various other areas.

In the summer of 1992, while I was ministering in Kensington Temple, my wife Ruth received a prophetic utterance which the pastor released her to give to the congregation. The Lord was speaking in the first person. His message began as follows:

I am the Lord. I have decided to visit London. Welcome Me with thanksgiving and praise. Honor Me by your godly conduct ....

Absolutely no glory shalt go to any human being. All the glory is Mine, and I will not share it with anyone.

There are four important points to notice.

First, the Lord declared His own Sovereign decision. It did not depend upon the people of London fulfilling certain conditions.

Second, the Lord spoke of "visiting" London. Probably what is taking place at present would most correctly be described as a "visitation." It would be premature to speak of "revival."

Third, the response that God requires from His people is "godly conduct."

Fourth, all the glory must go to the Lord.

Recently, I have received enquiries from many people—primarily in Britain—asking how we should evaluate these new and unfamiliar developments and how we should respond to them. Up to this time I myself have not been directly exposed to what is taking place. I will therefore limit myself to outlining a number of general principles which would apply in various different situations.

First of all, we need to recognize the fact that when an experience is unconventional—or even extraordinary—does not necessarily mean that it is not from God. In the Old Testament God required His prophets to do some extraordinary things. Isaiah had to walk naked and barefoot for three years (see Isaiah 20:1-3). Ezekiel was required to lie 390 days on his left side and 40 days on his right side, and then to prepare his food on a fire of cow dung (see Ezekiel 4:4-15).

In the Gospels Jesus Himself healed a deaf mute by spitting and touching his tongue (see Mark 7:32-35). Later, He healed a blind man by making clay from His own spittle and then smearing it on the blind man's eyes (see John 9:6-7). Further on, in the book of Acts, many things that took place in the early church would be considered highly unconventional in much of today's church.

It is appropriate, therefore, to approach unusual manifestations with caution, but not with blank, negative skepticism.

Whenever the church moves into the realm of the supernatural, it opens up exciting new possibilities of ministry, but it also exposes us to new forms of danger. The Bible clearly indicates—and church history abundantly confirms—that Satan is fully at home in the supernatural realm and that he prepares special traps and snares for Christians who move into this realm. In particular, in dealing with "the last days," the danger against which the Bible most persistently warns us is that of deception. We are instructed to **"test all things; to hold fast that which is good" (I Thessalonians 5:21).**

What sort of people do we need to be if we are to apply the appropriate tests? The answer is in Hebrews 5:14: **"But solid food is for the mature, who by constant use have trained themselves to distinguish good from evil" (NIV).**

There are two requirements: First, we must continually practice discernment in every situation that we encounter. The old saying, "practice makes perfect," applies in the spiritual realm as much as in the natural. Discernment must become as much a part of our spiritual walk as prayer or church attendance.

Second, we must cultivate a diet of solid spiritual food. A superficial acquaintance with a few familiar passages of Scripture is not enough. We must build a solid foundation of the great central doctrines of the Christian faith and learn how they apply to the various situations we encounter. Being a Christian is a full time job!

One critical area for discernment is the division between that which is spiritual and that which is soulish. Unfortunately, for many English readers the reality of this division is obscured by inconsistencies in translation from the original Greek. The Greek word for "spiritual" is *pneumatikos*, formed directly from *pneuma*, the word for "spirit." Exactly corresponding, the Greek word for "soulish" is *psuchikos*, formed directly from *psuche*, the word for "soul."

In English, *pneumatikos* is always translated "spiritual." Correspondingly, the natural translation for *psuchikos* would be "soulish." But since this is not a normal English word, various other words are used–e.g. "natural," or "carnal," or "worldly," or "sensual."

The problem is that these different translations give the impression that different Greek words are used. They tend to obscure two facts: First, that soulish is an important and distinctive New Testament concept. Second, that the soulish and the spiritual are often in conflict with one another.

The soul is the area in which man's natural reason and emotions function. This is quite different from the way that man's regenerated spirit is designed to function.

The contrast—and in fact, the opposition—between the two is clearly brought out in I Corinthians 2:14, 15:

> **But the natural [soulish] man does not receive the things of the Spirit of God, for they are foolishness to him; nor can he know them, because they are spiritually discerned.**
>
> **But he who is spiritual judges all things ....**

The conclusion is clear. Both the spiritual and the soulish man are found among the people of God. The spiritual man is at home in the things of the Holy Spirit and responds appropriately to them. On the other hand, the soulish man cannot apprehend the things of the Holy Spirit, but by his reaction distorts and debases them.

The only instrument sharp enough and sensitive enough to distinguish between the spiritual and the soulish is the word of God.

For the word of God is living and powerful and sharper than any two-edged sword, piercing even to the division of soul and spirit, and of joints and marrow, and is a discerner of the thoughts and intents of the heart (Hebrews 4:12).

This is why correct discernment is possible only for Christians who have become mature through regular feeding on the "solid food" of Scripture.

The failure to distinguish between the spiritual and the soulish can have disastrous consequences. Speaking of a certain kind of wisdom found among Christians, James says:

This wisdom does not descend from above, but is earthly [on the earthly plane], sensual [soulish], demonic (James 3:15).

James points out three stages in a disastrous decline. When Christians move out of the realm of the truly spiritual and descend to the earthly, it is then all too easy to move from that to the soulish, and from the soulish to the demonic. Experiences or manifestations which were initially spiritual become an open door for the activity of demons. All too often, however, Christians do not realize that they have passed from the realm of the spiritual through the soulish to the demonic.

Here is one example. Exuberant, hilarious joy can be a precious work of the Holy Spirit. God is delighted when His people delight themselves in Him. He loves a hilarious giver (see II Corinthians 9:7). But sometimes Christians can take their eyes off the Lord and begin to focus on their own subjective experiences. Their goal becomes their own personal enjoyment and their worship becomes a form of entertainment. In the end, true joy is replaced by frivolity and flippancy.

If we take Jesus as our pattern, however, we can find no trace of frivolity or flippancy in Him. Throughout His earthly life He never lost sight of the purpose for which He had come to earth: to save sinful men and women from the eternal agony of the lake of fire. All His teaching was permeated with the solemnity of eternal issues. He wept and He groaned, but He never jested. The same seriousness should permeate all that we do as Christians—and never more than when we are worshipping our Savior.

When our religion becomes play, we are on the verge of idolatry. It was said of the Israelites at the foot of Mount Sinai that **"the people sat down to eat and to drink, and rose up to play" (Exodus 32:6).** They had forgotten the awe-inspiring words that they had heard there from the mouth of God Himself. Their worship became a form of play, and the next stage was demonic—the worship of the golden calf. If our worship takes on the character of play, the result will be no less serious for us today.

Another way that the soulish nature expresses itself is in putting human leaders in a place that is reserved for Jesus alone.

It is right to express gratitude and appreciation to human ministers who have helped us, but never to offer them a kind of soulish adulation that borders on idolatry.

Years ago I knew a godly and successful pastor in Sweden who had built the largest Pentecostal church in Europe at that time. From time to time he would say to his congregation, "Please don't put me on a pedestal—because if you do, God will have to let me fall."

In recent years we have seen a whole succession of charismatic personalities who have ended in disaster for the simple reason that they allowed their followers to put them on a pedestal. The Lord is a jealous God. He has said, **"I will not give My glory to another" (Isaiah 48:11).**

Another danger that threatens those who minister in the supernatural realm is the temptation to use spiritual gifts to manipulate or exploit or dominate people. At one period in my ministry I found myself casting spirits of witchcraft out of church-going people. Eventually I asked the Lord to show me the true nature of witchcraft.

I believe that the Lord gave me the following definition: *Witchcraft is the attempt to control people and get them to do what you want by the use of any spirit that is not the Holy Spirit.*

After I had digested this, the Lord added: *And if anyone has a spirit that he can use, it is not the Holy Spirit.* The Holy Spirit is God, and no one uses God.

Today, I tremble inwardly when I see or hear of a person who claims that he has spiritual gifts which he is free to use just as he pleases. It is surely no accident that some of those who have made such claims have ended in serious doctrinal error.

I have given above three examples of dangers that result from confusing the soulish with the spiritual, but more could be added. What is important, is to cultivate a sensitivity to this issue, so that we are not deceived into accepting the soulish as if it were spiritual.

Paul wrote to the Philippian Christians:

And this I pray that your love may abound in true knowledge and discernment, so that you may distinguish between the things which differ, in order to be sincere and blameless until the day of Christ... (Philippians 1:9, 10 NAS Margin).

This is a prayer that we especially need to pray at this time, for ourselves and for one another.

In Matthew 7:16 Jesus gives a test to be applied to all ministries: **"You shall know them by their fruits."** Then in verses 17 and 18 He goes on to make a more specific application: **"Even so, every good tree bears good fruit, but a bad tree bears bad fruit. A good tree cannot bear bad fruit, nor can a bad tree bear good fruit."**

We need to make a practical application of this teaching of Jesus. Whenever we encounter bad fruit, we must recognize that it was produced by a bad tree. Therefore we need to discern and deal with the bad tree that produced the bad fruit.

But we need to go further. We need to recognize the kind of soil that produces bad trees: *It is pride.*

It was pride that caused Satan's downfall from heaven, and pride is the primary weapon that he uses to bring about the downfall of humanity. Therefore the only sure safeguard against deception and error is to cultivate humility.

Here again, Jesus is our pattern for self-humbling. In Philippians 2:5-8 Paul traces the seven successive downward steps that took Jesus from a place of equality with God to the death of a criminal on a cross. Then he continues: **"Therefore, God also has highly exalted Him...."**

Notice the significance of the "Therefore." Jesus was not exalted because He was a favorite Son. He was exalted because He had fulfilled the condition for being exalted—He had humbled Himself.

In Luke 14:11 Jesus affirms this as a general principle that applies throughout the universe: **"For whoever exalts himself will be humbled, and he who humbles himself will be exalted."**

God leaves it to each one of us to make our own decision. Shall we exalt ourselves and be abased? Or shall we humble ourselves and be exalted? If we make the right decision, we can move forward confidently into all that God is doing by His Holy Spirit, without fear of being deceived or going into error.

Unfortunately, however, Christians sometimes interpret some form of supernatural manifestation they have received as a badge of special spirituality. They tend to see themselves as being on a higher spiritual level than others who have not received a similar experience. The end result could be yet another tragic division in the Body of Christ between those who have had a certain kind of supernatural experience and those who have not.

Early in this century something similar resulted from the restoration of the gift of tongues to God's people. Christians were divided between those who spoke in tongues and those who did not. By the mercy of God this particular division is now on the way to being healed. Let us pray that it will not be succeeded by a fresh division over some other supernatural manifestation.

The Fruit We Should Look For

I have been emphasizing the principle that "a tree is known by its fruit." Logically, therefore, in evaluating the current move in the church, we should ask: If this move is from God, what kind of fruits should we look for? In reply, I would suggest five main kinds of fruit that would authenticate the present move.

1. The Fruit of Repentance

All through the New Testament the first thing that God demanded was not faith, but repentance. John the Baptist prepared the way for Jesus by calling for repentance (see Matthew 3:2). When religious people came to him for baptism, he demanded that they first produce in their lives the fruits of repentance (see Matthew 3:7-8).

The first word that Jesus preached was, "Repent" (see Mark 1:15). He told the multitudes **"Unless you repent, you will perish" (Luke 13:3-5).** After His resurrection He told His disciples that repentance, first, and then forgiveness of sins should be preached to all nations (see Luke 24:47).

On the day of Pentecost the first demand that Peter made of the convicted, but unconverted, multitude was "repent"—then be baptized. (Acts 2:38)

Speaking to the people of Athens, Paul said, **"God now commands all men everywhere to repent" (Acts 17:30).** Throughout his ministry he required, first repentance toward God, then faith toward Christ. (see Acts 20:21)

True repentance is not an emotion, but a decision of the will—a decision to turn away from all sin and unrighteousness and to submit unreservedly to the Lordship of Jesus.

Repentance is the first of the six foundation doctrines listed in Hebrews 6:1-2. Those who have not truly repented can never have a solid foundation for their lives as Christians. Over the years I have counseled hundreds of Christians with various problems in their lives. As a result, I have concluded that at least 50 per cent of the problems in the lives of Christians are due to one simple fact: they have never truly repented.

I believe that a renewed emphasis on repentance is the most urgent need of the contemporary church in the West. To be effective, any move in the church must deal with this issue.

2. Respect for Scripture

A second decisive factor in our lives as Christians is our attitude to Scripture. Jesus called the Scripture "the word of God," and He set His personal seal upon it by five simple words: **"the Scripture cannot be broken" (John 10:35).** No amount of "higher criticism" can set aside the plain meaning of these words. If we believe in Jesus then we believe in the Bible. If we do not believe in the Bible, then we do not believe in Jesus.

In Isaiah 66:2 the Lord says: **"This is the one I esteem: he who is humble and contrite in spirit, and trembles at my word" (NIV).** God here combines repentance—a humble and contrite spirit—with faith in His word.

Why should we tremble at God's word? First, because it is the way that God the Father and God the Son come to us and make their home with us (see John 14:23). Second, because God's word will one day be our judge (see John 12:48).

From creation onwards, God has worked through two main agents: His word and His Spirit. First, the Spirit of God moved: then God's word went forth (see Genesis 1:2, 3). The result was creation.

Ever since then the Spirit and the word have always worked together in harmony. Anything that the Spirit does harmonizes with what the word says. Furthermore, all Scripture is inspired by His Holy Spirit and He never contradicts Himself (see II Timothy 3:16).

This means that every kind of spiritual manifestation must be tested by this standard: Is it in harmony with Scripture? If so, we can receive it. If not, we must reject it.

3. Exaltation of Jesus

In John 16:13, 14 Jesus promised His disciples, **"When He, the Spirit of truth has come, He will guide you into all truth.... He will glorify Me...."**

Jesus here reveals two important facts about the ministry of the Holy Spirit. First of all, His supreme function is to glorify Jesus. This provides an authoritative test of any spiritual manifestation. Does it focus our attention on Jesus? Does it exalt Jesus?

As soon as human personalities are allowed to take the center of the stage, the

Holy Spirit begins to withdraw. The exaltation of human personalities has many times quenched what was originally a genuine move of the Holy Spirit.

Then we need to notice that Jesus is careful to emphasize that the Holy Spirit is not an "it" but a "He." When people begin to explain spiritual experience in terms of getting "it," it can easily happen that they get the wrong "it."

Jesus is a person and the Holy Spirit is a person. The Holy Spirit, as a person, draws believers together around the person of Jesus. When we make a doctrine or an experience the focus of our gathering, we are spiritually "off center."

4. Love for Our Fellow Christians

In John 13:35 Jesus told His followers, **"By this all will know that you are My disciples, if you have love for one another."** In I Timothy 1:5 Paul said, **"The goal of our instruction is love from a pure heart and a good conscience and sincere faith" (NAS).** Any form of religious activity that does not produce this result, he dismissed as "fruitless discussion."

In I Corinthians 13:2, Paul applied this test to himself: **"If I have all the spiritual gifts of power and of revelation, but have not love, I am nothing."**

Before we apply this test to others, we need to do the same as Paul and apply it to ourselves. We each need to ask: Has my faith made me a loving person?

Then—and only then—can we apply this test to the present move in the church. Is it producing Christians who sincerely love one another—regardless of denominational labels? Will it cause the unbelievers to say of these people what the world said of the early church; "See how these Christians love one another?"

5. Loving Concern for the Unreached

In John 4:35, Jesus told His disciples, **"Lift up your eyes and look at the fields, for they are white already for harvest."** If those words were true even in the time of Jesus, they are certainly more true today. I have been privileged to travel and minister in many nations and I have formed one firm conclusion: *We are living in the harvest hour!*

Yet, alas, many Christians, who could be working in the harvest fields of the world, are caught in a snare of materialistic self-centeredness. I believe that any genuine move of the Holy Spirit will result in multitudes of new laborers being thrust forth into the world's harvest fields. Otherwise it does not truly reflect the heart of God.

If a significant number of Christians in the current move successfully pass all, or most, of the five tests outlined above, then it is safe to conclude that this is, essentially, a move of God. This does not mean that everyone or everything in it is faultless.God has no faultless people to work with. It is amazing what He can do with weak and fallible people who are truly surrendered to Him. ∎

Derek Prince was educated in Britain at Eton and King's College, Cambridge. Later he held a Fellowship in Philosophy at King's. He now heads a ministry that provides Bible teaching material in many languages to 140 nations through books, audio and video cassettes, and radio and television broadcasts. This article, as well as a catalog of other products can be ordered from DPMI, P.O. Box 19501, Charlotte, NC 28219-9501, Phone: (704)357-3556.

A PROPHETIC LESSON

by

DAVID WHITE

PROPHECY

All Scriptures NKJV.

As the end of this age draws nearer, the Lord's heart will become increasingly known to those who seek to know Him, and make it their aim to please Him. We can no longer afford to major on what God might consider a minor, and minor on what He would consider a major. If we are going to bring pleasure to God, and see His glory in our generation, we must focus on the interests of the King.

To do this we need to know what is on God's heart, and what is on His mind. God spoke this prophetically to Eli when he said, **"Then I will raise up for Myself a faithful priest who shall do according to what is in My heart and in My mind" (I Samuel 2:35).** Although this was fulfilled after the death of Eli's sons, there is coming a greater fulfillment of this promise in the last days. In fact, it is no longer an option, but is imperative that we both know God's agenda and be actively involved with it continually.

How can we, as individual members of the Body of Christ, discover and become actively involved each day with God's agenda? Recently the Lord walked me through an experience that may help answer this question.

It was a beautiful sunny afternoon in southwest Pennsylvania. My brother-in-law and I were in his car driving on a hilly, winding country road. Suddenly we came upon something neither of us wanted to see. The road was blocked and a number of emergency and medical personnel had already arrived. We got out of the car for a closer look, and to see if we might be of some assistance.

As we approached the scene, I saw what was probably the worst accident I had ever seen. Two cars had met in a head on collision. Immediately after we walked up to where we could see what was happening, a car pulled up behind us. It was the coroner. When he got out of the car he was met by a law enforcement official who said to him, "We have two fatalities." The coroner then opened his trunk, and removed two body bags. Then, as one of the injured was being taken away, we saw two bodies lying on the grass beside the road.

This accident had occurred in front of a high school, and a large number of students were lined up along the roadside watching the entire scene as it unfolded. At that moment, this thought arose in my mind, *"Pray that the students learn what they are supposed to learn."*

My heart sank as I saw the coroner lift the sheets from the bodies of a young boy and a girl, who both looked to be in their mid to late teens. The coroner then began to take the necessary photographs for their records, and I was sure, the newspapers. As this was happening, I began to ask the Lord what I could do to help, forgetting the thought that had previously arisen in my mind.

Then I thought, "what a great opportunity for a miracle, a resurrection." I told the Lord how this was an excellent opportunity for a public display of His power over death. If God raised these two teenagers from the dead in front of all these students, I just knew that revival would begin and spread across all of Pennsylvania. My heart was also just bleeding for all those involved in this horrible scene.

Then I began to search my heart for something upon which I could base my desire to see a resurrection. Had I dreamed where God had used me to raise the dead? Did I receive a word of knowledge about such an experience? Did I sense an anointing, or the gift of faith rising up to do such an act? I even shared with my brother-in-law my willingness to go over and pray for these two that God would raise them up. However, I confessed that I really could not point to anything that I was certain to be a word from God to do anything.

With a broken heart, I left feeling there was nothing else I could do. As we drove off, I wondered if I had missed an opportunity to see a miracle. Could those two teenagers have been saved if I had just had the faith? All I could do was pray that God would show up in the midst of that horrible tragedy and somehow be glorified.

When we arrived at our destination, I asked someone if he had heard about the accident that had occurred just up the road. I then found out that the two young people, who had been lying on the side of the road were now alive. In fact, they never died!

What we witnessed was a mock accident scene! Prom night was less than two weeks away and the authorities were trying to impress upon these students the dangers of drinking and driving. When I heard the news, a sense of relief came over me, not only for the teenagers, but for me! I was so glad that I did not walk over to the bodies, raise up the sheet and pray for a resurrection. Those two would have gotten up, and they probably would have had to take me away in the ambulance instead.

I thanked God that I didn't make a mockery of His power in doing something so foolish when He had not instructed me to do so. It was not long after this, that God reminded me that He did speak to me within moments after I had arrived at the scene. He had told me simply to pray that the students learn what it was they were supposed to learn. I was looking for a resurrection; God was looking for education.

As a result of this experience, I believe God taught me some valuable lessons regarding hearing and obeying His voice, and how we might discover and become involved with His agenda on a day by day, even a moment by moment basis.

First, in discovering and doing God's agenda, we must act on the commands of God rather than on human compassion. When Jesus received news of the death of His friend Lazarus, the scripture says, "... **He stayed two more days in the place where He was" (John 11:6).** We know that Jesus loved Lazarus; however, He was not led by compassion, He was led by what He saw the Father doing. The power of God accompanies the Word of God, and not necessarily the compassion of man. Human compassion can even be a stumbling block in fulfilling God's purposes. **"For as many as are led by the Spirit of God, these are sons of God" (Romans 8:14).**

"True ministry is not just something we receive from the Lord, but its that which we receive in the Lord."

Second, to discover and act on God's agenda we must live each day with a sense of expectation rather than experimentation. Jesus never experimented on people to see if He could discover what God would do. He only did what the Father was doing at the moment. The hit and miss approach to ministry will result in more misses than hits. God didn't call us to be scientists, experimenting to see what works—He called us to be sons. He called us as sons whose expectation is in the Lord, who believe in who He is, not simply betting on what He can do.

When the Apostle Paul spoke concerning Archippus, a fellow servant of the Lord, he said, **"Take heed to the ministry which you have received *in* the Lord, that you may fulfill it" (Colossians 4:17).** True ministry is not just something we receive from the Lord, but its that which we receive *in* the Lord. True ministry comes from a daily walking out of our relationship of being *in Christ*.

Third, to discover and become involved in God's agenda, our focus must be in our knowledge of Him, not in our knowledge of the problem. At the beginning of this decade, I asked the Lord for a scripture verse on which I could stand throughout the entire ten years, that would sum up what He wanted to do. The verse He gave me was, **"..but the people *who know their God* shall be strong, and carry out great exploits" (Daniel 11:32).** Doing great exploits was and is exciting; yet doing the great exploits comes only as we continue to know God.

Paul said, **"Now thanks be to God who always leads us in triumph in Christ, and through us diffuses the fragrance of His knowledge in every place" (II Corinthians 2:14).** Today, in the church we have experts in the area of church growth, experts in children's ministry, experts in counseling, experts in preaching, experts in fundraising. However, there is truly only one expert in the church, and He's the Head of the Body. Effective ministry does not automatically come from our knowledge of someone's problem, but rather from our knowledge of God.

Fourth, to discover and become involved with God's agenda, we must resist the desire to replace inactivity with our own activity. The desire to "do something for God," can actually distract us from doing the thing He has called us to do. It has been said that God does not appreciate what He does not initiate. Inactivity does not mean we're missing out. Instead, it is

continued on page 85

JUDGING PROPHECY

PROPHECY

by

KEITH HAZELL

All Scriptures NIV unless otherwise noted.

Now, brothers, about times and dates we do not need to write to you (I Thessalonians 5:1).

June 9, 1994, was prophesied to be the day when evil would be ripped out of the earth; yet it came and went and the world still seems to be the same. There is no apparent change either in action, attitude or aspect in our sick and sad world. Some Charismatics were disappointed and dismayed that what they had anticipated has not come to pass. Not a few of their Evangelical brothers remain puzzled that so many Charismatic believers could be so easily distraught over such bizarre things.

Charismatic believers, especially on this continent, have consistently shown that they are susceptible to apocalyptic and bizarre predictions concerning the ultimate end of all things. I expect that we will eventually hear from the people that originated the "rip the evil out" prediction for June 9, 1994, that it did actually occur "in the heavenlies." We will "have our faith renewed" once more to believe that the things we long to see are actually happening in some hidden dimension.

When I commented publicly that I doubted the credibility of the June 9th prophecy, I was told by some that I was resisting a word from the Holy Spirit. Others thought it inadvisable to speak against such things in public. However, we have proven ourselves too willing to believe, too credulous, too ready to clutch at any straw that promises it will make anything we do not like go away quickly (with as little work on our part as possible). In the process we open ourselves to deception on a massive scale.

Just a few years ago a substantial number of Christians, both Charismatics and others, believed that the world would end in 1988. Anyone who spoke contrary was considered to be unspiritual. A subsequent amendment to the following year in no way daunted those who felt they would soon be openly vindicated. Very few of the prominent leaders in the Charismatic-type stream of Christian expression publicly refuted these predictions. Not wanting to "lift their hand against the Lord's anointed" they chose rather to hide behind "prudence." Alternatively they felt they should keep out of the controversy. This conveniently dodges or ignores Ezekiel's comments regarding God holding the watchmen responsible if they do not cry out when danger to the church is present. It remains a mystery to me that the prophetic men and women in our churches can "cry out against Babylon" but cannot, or will not, speak with clarity about events happening in our own backyard.

Paul had similar problems with the church in his day. People were constantly being harassed by those claiming revelation concerning the second coming or some other apocalyptic event.

... We ask you, brothers, not to become easily unsettled or alarmed by some prophecy, report or letter supposed to have come from us, saying that the day of the Lord has already come (II Thessalonians 2:1, 2).

Such a preoccupation made them fail to plan for the future. It made them to be continually in the state of alarm. Doesn't this sound familiar? Paul had to write to the church and warn them not to become destabilized. **"So then, brothers, stand firm and hold to the teachings we passed on to you, whether by word of mouth or by letter" (II Thessalonians 2:15).**

Why are we so susceptible? Why do we wish to have a quick way out? Our problem is that we have outlived our eschatology (doctrine of end times) and are desperately hoping to correct our situation with wishful thinking. Many of us who were touched by the Holy Spirit in the 60's and 70's believed then that Jesus would have returned long before now. On top of this disappointment, we have suffered the distasteful disenchantment of witnessing some celebrated Christian leaders publicly disgraced for sexual immorality. Great institutions which arose in this same era are now being liquidated or sold off at reduced prices. With all of this has come a sense of inability to represent Christ to a society which has largely rejected "Television Christianity."

Proverbs 29:18 states: **"Where there is no revelation the people cast off restraint."** We often think of applying this to the heathen, but it has a strong application to the church in North America in the 90's. Paul, writing in II Timothy 4:3, points to the very situation we are now experiencing:

For the time will come when men will not put up with sound doctrine. Instead, to suit their own desires, they will gather around them a great number of teachers to say what their itching ears want to hear.

We are living in a day that men are frustrated looking for direction in a church that has collectively lost its way. So how should we respond to such predictions? There are several points I would like to ask you to consider.

1. When God is speaking a prediction to the Church (a word for all believers) we should expect to hear a consistent message across the whole Body from recognized prophets, not "echoes." Amos 3:7 states: **"Surely the Sovereign Lord does nothing without revealing his plan to his servants the prophets."** That is *prophets*— plural.

2. When God reveals what He is going to do in judgment, He is usually specific. He is not esoteric—speaking only to the inner circle. Nor is He vague or undefined in His statements like fortune cookies and horoscopes that can be interpreted any number of ways. For example, God spoke very clearly to Joseph of His intentions regarding Israel and Egypt. Noah was told about the flood. Sodom was warned in clear and practical terms.

3. When God is going to judge or bring catastrophe on a nation, He often gives special instructions for the protection of His people. The Israelites escaped the judgment of the death angel in Egypt by obeying God's warning to put the blood of a lamb on the doorpost of their houses. Noah had a specific word about boat building to protect himself and his family from the coming flood.

4. Prophetic words of this nature are usually a confirmation to the leaders in the body of Christ. If they are not confirmation they should not be accepted and promoted until they have been searched out and judged to be from the Lord.

We must not become cynical about the prophetic, throwing the baby out with the bath water. Yet we must not get caught up in every wind of prophecy or teaching that comes our way, allowing everyone who is looking for a platform to share their "revelation." We must operate on the sound biblical principles concerning judgment of prophecy or the sheep entrusted to our care will continue to be confused and distracted. We must avoid the caustic cynicism of rejecting the prophetic on the one

"We are living in a day that men are frustrated looking for direction in a church that has collectively lost its way."

extreme, as well as the blind gullibility of believing everything that comes along.

Most churches have a three year plan. Some have a five year plan. What about a fifty year plan? Instead of planning for the future, making long range strategies that will affect generations, we diffuse our energies debating the details of different endtime theories. What we believe about the endtimes, especially the imminence of the second coming of Christ, will affect how we prepare and plan for the future. While some of us have made some long range plans for our families (buying a house with a twenty year mortgage, saving for our child's college expenses, just in case Jesus doesn't return next week) we have not felt it "spiritually correct" to have long range plans in the church.

I am not suggesting that we do not believe in the return of Christ, but I am suggesting that belief in the return of Christ does not relieve us of our responsibilities as stewards of the time we do have. We have all missed opportunities in the past because of our short sightedness. If we had known back in 1975 that Jesus would not return prior to 1994 we would have planned differently. Jesus, speaking to the eschatologists of His day, in a parable instructed them to **"occupy till I come" (Luke 19:13 KJV)**. When He spoke this He was not talking about finding something to entertain yourself with while waiting for the bus to arrive. Rather it carries with it the thought of being gainfully employed while facing uncertain conditions.

What of the future of the church? What must we face in the years ahead? Should we be planning and preparing or passively letting the future continue to take us by surprise? In our society we have people described as futurists who devote their resources to discovering what the future trends are going to be in business and commerce and life in general. We need Holy Spirit anointed "futurists" in the church who will help guide and develop our plans—prophetic voices which not only speak of floods but of how to build large boats. There is coming a harvest that some have described as a flood. We need to have God's wisdom and direction in mobilizing laborers, developing strategies, training workers, insuring the availability and condition of proper equipment, acquiring needed facilities and selling any unnecessary facilities.

Joseph was a man who God enabled to bring practical direction to Egypt. The Spirit of God gave Joseph a fourteen year plan. God showed him a clear picture of what was going to happen and how to prepare for it. Would God help us to have similar insights? Agabus (see Acts 11:28) predicted a coming famine that would affect the whole Roman world. This prediction enabled the church to meet the future prepared. They collected money on the strength of that prediction. Where are those that will help the church today to do this? Is there a fear that predictive prophecy will get out of hand? Do we actually believe there is a future? If we believe there is no future, then we should sell our buildings, our homes and all we possess.

We could reinvest it all in promoting the gospel.

The future requires strategies based, not on our observations of the current trends, but on actual revelation from the One who holds the future. Christianity stands like a bewildered man at a bus stop. He has just watched the bus he intended to catch go off in the opposite direction. I believe that instead of "deep" and unintelligible promises of things that cannot be proven, prophecy needs to be plain and practical so the church can prepare. There are still nations to be reached with the gospel. We need strategic planning with wisdom to reach them.

Paul had intentions to go into Bithynia but was restrained by the Spirit of Jesus. God revealed His intentions and showed Paul, in a dream, a Macedonian. God gave Paul a nation. Peter, when faced with people he didn't especially want to reach—the Gentiles, responded to God's prophetic revelation which came in a trance. He went to the House of Cornelius and was used of God to open the door of the Kingdom to an unreached people group. Ananias (not the one who God executed) received revelation to go to a street called Straight. Saul of Tarsus sat there in darkness waiting for deliverance. Ananias was moved by God's instruction to do something that he was reluctant to do and, as a result, a man was reached that affected the destiny of nations for Jesus. Prophetic revelation has always held a very important place in God's direction for His people, and it still does today, but it must be handled according to His instructions.

> *"The future requires strategies based, not on our observations of the current trends, but on actual revelation from the One who holds the future."*

continued on page 86

THE POWER OF THE HOLY SPIRIT

by
PAUL CAIN & RICK JOYNER

PROPHECY

All Scriptures KJV unless otherwise noted.

The prophet Zechariah exhorts us to understand what is becoming one of the most crucial truths of our time: **"Not by might, nor by power, but by My Spirit, saith the Lord of hosts!" (Zechariah 4:6).** We are approaching the time when the church will indeed understand this truth, and will live by it.

The Holy Spirit is the only Source of the power that is required for the church to accomplish her purposes. Human influence, resources, wisdom, and will power are all totally inadequate. Even the best education will not guarantee us success. These can all be useful in their proper place, but they can hinder us greatly if they are not kept in their proper place.

With all of our modern tools and props, a church service can be powerfully appealing and able to draw multitudes, completely without the Holy Spirit. Will this ever accomplish the purposes of God? Even the best intentions of men cannot remake men—only the Holy Spirit can.

We do not need more resources to accomplish the will of God, we need more men going back to the Source.

Lasting Fruit

This is not to imply that we should abandon all modern tools for promoting the gospel. Many of the truly effective spiritual movements in history made full use of modern inventions. The Reformation was propelled and expanded by the invention of the printing press. But, we must understand that we cannot accomplish one thing that will produce truly lasting fruit without the Holy Spirit. Jesus said in John 15:5: **"I am the vine, you are the branches; he who abides in Me, and I in him, he bears much fruit;** *for apart from Me you can do nothing."*

The true work of God will always start with the Holy Spirit, who may then direct the use of other tools. However, when we try to first build a ministry with the other tools, and then we ask Him to come and bless it, it is improbable that we will have built something that He can use. As Paul told the men of Athens: **"The God who** made the world and all things in it, since He is Lord of heaven and earth, does not dwell in temples made with hands; neither is He served by human hands…" **(Acts 17:24, 25a).** The quality of our spiritual fruitfulness will depend upon the degree to which the Holy Spirit both started and finished the work. Jesus is both the Alpha and Omega, the Beginning and the End. He will not be just one or the other.

Modern man does not just need reform—he needs regeneration. Changes in morality can be good, but if they are not the result of reconciliation with God, they can work to make man's path to destruction smoother and easier, and the way to true life more difficult to find. There can be a major difference between trying to make men better and reconciling them to God. The former can still have its origin in The Tree of the Knowledge of Good and Evil. The "good" side of this tree can be an even more deadly enemy than the evil side because it is much more deceptive—it becomes a substitute for the Tree of Life, Jesus Christ.

The Lord is not just trying to keep men from sinning—He is trying to deliver them from what causes the sin. If we convince someone that it is in his best interest to change his morality, he will quickly change his morality back again when it appears to serve his interests. True change goes beyond changing minds to changing hearts. The Lord even had to warn the great prophet Samuel about this saying, **"Do not look at his appearance or at the height of his stature, because I have rejected him; for God sees not as man sees, for man looks at the outward appearance, but the Lord looks at the heart"** (I Samuel 16:7).

When our hearts have been changed we will not be so blown about by the winds of expediency. That is why the Lord declared that unless we are born again to have a fundamental change of life, we cannot even see the kingdom of God.

We're Here to Overthrow a Kingdom

It is much better to influence men to live according to moral standards than immoral ones, but the Lord gave His church the Holy Spirit to do much more than this. It is written that Jesus came to destroy the works of the devil (see I John 3:8). He also stated that, as He was sent into the world, He has sent us (see John 17:18). Every Christian is here on earth to destroy the works of the enemy. It is not enough for us to just try to change the moral climate of our cities or nations, we must cast down the enemy's strongholds, destroying them so that they cannot be rebuilt.

We are not warring against flesh and blood. We will never displace the evil influences over this world with human brilliance or strength. **"For the weapons of our warfare are not carnal, but mighty through God, to the pulling down of strongholds" (II Corinthians 10:4).** Anything less than this will never bear lasting fruit. We can use political or other pressures to persuade men to change their behavior for a time, but as soon as the pressures are removed the shallowness of the change becomes apparent. As the Lord said, **"But if I cast out demons by the Spirit of God, then the kingdom of God has come upon you" (Matthew 12:28).** Only the Spirit of God can cast out demons. Anything less than casting the enemy out is ultimately an exercise in futility. We are not here to make Satan's kingdom more livable—we are here to overthrow his kingdom!

Mountains of Trouble

When Zechariah exhorted the remnant in the name of the Lord not to trust in might and power, but in the Spirit, they were facing impossible problems. They were standing in front of a huge mountain of rubble that had been the city of Jerusalem and the temple before its overthrow. All of their neighbors hated them and were spreading slander about them, as well as physically threatening them. The faithful were few in number; they were discouraged and weak. Any one of their problems looked humanly impossible to overcome—and they were! But they served a God who delighted in turning mountains into plains, who loved to raise up the valleys and low places—and a God who truly is *all powerful*!

Today the church finds herself being pressed on every side as never before. Evil is taking over the government, the schools, and seemingly every other human institution. At the same time the church seemingly lies in a pile of rubble with hardly a hint of her former glory visible. We too are faced with an impossible task, but that is precisely where the Lord does His best work.

Our task is already beyond human might and power. Our candidates may win an election here and there, and we may place a few people on the school boards, or even on the Supreme Court, which are certainly worthwhile endeavors, but the overwhelming tide of evil does not seem to have been affected very much. Our candidates can win all of the elections, we can place all of our judges on the courts, but the demonic powers we are facing do not

care about laws. God did not come to win elections and He has not sent us to win them. The kingdom of God will not come by popular vote. When the enemy comes in like a flood, the Spirit of the Lord will raise up a standard against him. The Lord and just one faithful man constitute a majority against any evil hoard.

The Fall Continues

It is a blind and backslidden church that gets more excited about a candidate than they do about Christ. It is a blind and backslidden church that puts more faith in a political party than in prayer. It is a blind and backslidden church that gives more time, effort and resources to politics than to the gospel. We can gain all of the political influence in the world and not accomplish a fraction as much as we would if we had influence with God. Satan would much rather have the church out campaigning than preaching the gospel. While we are so distracted, the world is slipping into deeper darkness. What is now happening to the world is happening on our watch! And it is not happening because we did not vote, but because we did not *pray.*

The disciples in the early church were noticed in a much more striking way, as we read in Acts 4:13: **"Now as they observed the confidence of Peter and John, and understood that they were uneducated and untrained men, they were marveling, and *began to recognize them as having been with Jesus*"** (NASB). The leaders of their day did not vote for them, but they did take note of them. Not because of their education or training, but *because they had been with Jesus.* Nothing will draw the world's attention to us in the proper way like simply spending time with Him. The more we are with Him, the more we will become like Him.

The only reason that we should want men to be drawn to us is because of Christ in us. If they are being drawn for any other reason, we are not serving as ambassadors of Christ, but of our own agenda. Satan learned well in the Garden that the best way to keep men from the Tree of Life is to get them to eat from the Tree of the Knowledge of Good and Evil. This continues to be one of his most effective strategies to bring death into the world.

Once a monk was pointing out to a great Christian leader the magnificent buildings and wealth that the medieval church had acquired, remarking: "Never again can we say, 'Silver and gold have I none.'" "That is true," replied the leader, "but neither can we say, 'In the name of Jesus, rise up and walk.'"

It is not wrong for Christians to be involved in politics. Christians do have a responsibility to be good citizens and to get involved. But we must understand that politics will never be the source of power that we need to accomplish our purpose on earth. We must not keep majoring on the minors. A prayer meeting that has authority with God can accomplish far more than any human congress. We have been given the authority to have that which we bind on earth, bound in heaven. We should pray for our governments, and we should support righteous men who are trying to influence government for the sake of righteousness. We must give to Caesar the things that are his, and give to God the things that are His. But if we are building our hope on Caesar (and many are), regardless of how well-intentioned they seem to be, we are in for a tragic disappointment.

The Lord has entrusted His church with a power that greatly exceeds that of any human government. The church must come to know and use the power that she has been given. Simple faith in God can move the hand of God, and that can accomplish more than all of the political maneuvering and campaigning the world has ever known.

If we have beheld the glory of our King we will surely understand that to be involved in earthly government is the low calling, not the high calling. One who has seen the King of Heaven will not be impressed with mere earthly kings or presidents. A pastor with two hundred sheep can have a greater impact on the world for righteousness than any political leader in the world. The key phrase here is "can have." The truth is that few have. This is no fault of the Word of God, but of our willingness to live by it.

The Power of Truth

We are coming to a time when there will be a people who believe the Word of God, and who live it. They will build their lives upon citizenship in another kingdom. Martin Luther is one of history's greatest examples of how just one humble man, who will take his stand and refuse to compromise his convictions, can push back the greatest darkness of his times. No conqueror, or Caesar, in history ever impacted the world the way that one monk did. His feat was accomplished from the obscure little village of Wittenburg, Germany, from a church that was not as big as most of our garages today.

The Lord is about to raise up a thousand Luthers who will shake this world to its foundations a thousand times. The few truths they nail to their little church doors will

accomplish far more than countless librar-
ies of human philosophies and theologies.
Kings and presidents will all tremble at the
power of their little pens. That is because
the power in their pens will not be the
words they write, but the anointing behind
them. The endorsement of the Holy Spirit
counts more than all of the political maneuvering and campaigning the world has
ever known.

Those who have put their trust in men's
chariots or horses have cast their vote for
the losing side, regardless of who they
voted for. We have a God who can pay
taxes by putting money in the mouth of a
fish. He can take a child's lunch and feed
a multitude; He never let the widow's
cruse of oil run out; surely He can provide
for us regardless of what the economy
does. The God who parted the Red Sea,
who calmed the storm and walked on the
waves, can protect us, and cause us to
prosper, regardless of what the weather does.

The God who moved upon the earth that
was formless and void, to bring forth such
a glorious creation, can bring order to your
life, and cause the world to marvel at the
glory He brings forth out of even the worst
confusion. The God who converted Saul
of Tarsus can take our worst persecutor and
turn him into one of the great heroes of the
faith. But He will not do any of this
through our wisdom or our strength, but by
His Spirit.

Another Pentecost

The faithful who draw together in unity,
devoting themselves to prayer and ministry to the Lord, will experience an end time
Day of Pentecost greater than the first. In
fact, the first Day of Pentecost was but a
token promise of what He will do at the
end. Just as was prophesied on the first
Day of Pentecost, in the last days the Lord
is going to pour out His Spirit on all flesh.
The Holy Spirit will again descend upon
the faithful with such glory and power that
men from every nation and tongue will
understand the message. The church that
was born in power will complete her mission in power. The wine that He has saved
for last will be even better than the first. In
the time of the world's deepest darkness,
the glory of the Lord will shine brightest.

Many sincere students of the Word have
been hindered by the way they have divided the prophecies of Scripture. They
mistakenly interpret many of the promises
as words for "after" the Lord's return. We
won't need them then! The Lord is coming
to the church before He comes *for* her. He
will have a bride without spot or wrinkle.
He will have a prophetic church that will
not compromise His word, and she will not
commit spiritual adultery with the ways of
the world. God will pour out His Spirit
without measure on a church without mixture.

Earthly power is frail and transient, but
a power from on high is coming that will
shake the powers of earth by revealing the
powers of heaven. Wait for it. Pray for it.
Do not settle for anything less than it. The
pressing needs of the time demand it. Our
glorious Savior deserves it.

**"Not by might, nor by power, but
by My Spirit," says the Lord of
hosts (Zechariah 4:6).** ◼

JON AMOS COMENIUS

by RICK JOYNER

All Scriptures NAS unless otherwise noted.

Jon Amos Comenius could be included on a short list of those who have had the most impact on the modern world. He is recognized as the father of modern education, and is still considered by many to be the greatest genius to ever work in that field. His contribution to the science of learning could be traced as a primary cause of the great and accelerating increase of knowledge that has been the hallmark of the last few centuries. What is not always remembered about him is that his great impact on the march of civilization was the result of his relentless passion to know the Son of God.

Comenius was born in Bohemia (now Czechoslovakia) in 1592. He was so quiet and shy that he was thought to be slightly retarded. However, there were deeper influences at work within him than were readily apparent. Born into the Moravian evangelical movement, he was touched early by a deep love for the Savior. However, Jon Amos hated his school and was therefore a slow learner. He suffered at the hands of cruel and thoughtless teachers. Later he would call those contemporary schools "slaughterhouses of the mind," believing that because of them most children began to hate books and literature. Even so, he persevered until he was able to attend the Calvinist University at Herborn. In 1614, he became a teacher at a Moravian school in Prerau. It was there that he introduced new teaching methods that would change the world.

The fuel that propelled Comenius' quest for knowledge was the belief that because all things were made through Christ and for Him (see Colossians 1:16), Christ could be seen in everything. He contended that all true knowledge would reveal the glory of Christ, declaring that *"nature is God's second book."* This passion became so contagious that much of the world was touched by it. Not only did he give birth to modern education, but some of the great revivals over the next four centuries could trace their origins to the seeds sown by this one man.

In 1618, Comenius became the pastor of a Moravian congregation in Fulneck which included his being in charge of its school. Soon the school at Fulneck became known throughout Moravia. It was during this time that he began to write extensively. However, dark clouds were gathering over Europe that would radically alter the direction of Comenius' life. The Thirty Years War began to unfold in such a way that it seemed as though it had been purposely directed to disrupt his great work.

In 1620, at the Battle of the White Mountain, the Catholics prevailed and Moravia officially became Catholic. Comenius was told that he could retain his school on the condition of renouncing his Moravian convictions. He refused. He then lost not only the school but also his precious library and all of his writings. As increasing murder, violence and hunger reduced the population from three million to one million, he also lost his wife and his only child.

Having suffered the worst tragedy that a loving husband and father could suffer, Comenius determined not to look down, but up. He felt that he now understood even more what a great sacrifice the Father had made in giving His Son for the sins of the world. He also knew even more deeply how desperately this fallen world needed the Savior, and he resolved to do all that he could to reveal Him.

In 1624, Comenius, the ever faithful pastor, led a small band of exiles out of their native land to seek a safe haven. He would remain a refugee for the rest of his life. War after war continued to erupt around him, always in such a way as to destroy much of his work. Time after time

"As increasing murder, violence and hunger reduced the population from three million to one million, he also lost his wife and his only child."

he would be driven from his home just when it seemed that the roots he was putting down were beginning to bear fruit. Even through this remarkable and continuous onslaught, this humble pastor and school teacher never became discouraged. He would just formulate an even greater plan to be implemented at his next destination. He was determined to see the world illuminated with the glory of his Savior, and he began to view this as possible through education.

The Prophecy

As Comenius and the little band of exiles left Moravia, he gave a remarkable, and now famous, prophecy. He told his followers that God would preserve "a hidden seed" which would grow and bear fruit *in a hundred years time.* John Hus (1369-1415), who was the spiritual father of the Reformation, and the first of the Moravian movement, had first prophesied concerning the "hidden seed" before being burned at the stake for his protests against Catholic tyranny. This prophecy had been kept alive in the hearts of the Moravians for over two hundred years, and Comenius declared that in another century it would sprout.

The Prophecy Leads to Strategy

To the modern church that is so bound by the "tyranny of the immediate," a prophecy that their hope would not be fulfilled for another hundred years would seem very discouraging. It actually had the opposite effect upon the Moravians. As a people devoted to self-sacrifice, they were honored to be able to help prepare the way for a future generation. This also enabled them to plan with such a long term strategy and vision that it made some of their greatest contributions to the church and civilization possible.

Taking his own prophecy to heart about the continued one hundred year dormancy of the seed, Comenius began to plan accordingly. Wanting to lay the strongest possible foundation for the future restoration of his people, he felt that the best way he could do this would be to dedicate his life entirely to the education of the young. One day, multiplied millions of the world's children would benefit from his plans.

> *"He knew beyond question that these were a people with a divine destiny."*

The Prophecy Fulfilled

One hundred years later Count Ludwick von Zinzendorf allowed a few Moravian refugees, from the movement that Comenius had perpetuated, haven on his estate. At that time, as he was studying in a nearby library, he happened upon the writings of Jon Amos Comenius. He was stunned by how accurately those writings articulated some of the deepest burdens of his own heart. He was amazed when he understood that this Comenius was a spiritual ancestor of the refugees he had just taken under his wing. Zinzendorf then read a list of disciplines instituted by Comenius for governing the community one hundred years earlier, that almost exactly paralleled a list of governing rules that he had just a few days prior given to the Moravian refugees. He knew beyond question that these were a people with a divine destiny.

That day in the library, a spark was ignited in the young nobleman that would not only forever change his life, but also the course of the entire advancing church. Zinzendorf quickly returned and encouraged the refugees with the words of Comenius. The result of that meeting is now recorded in history as "The Moravian Pentecost."

The Moravian community was established at Herrnhut in 1722, and the "Moravian Pentecost" occurred in August 1727. After one hundred years the seed had sprung to life, and one of the great Christian movements of all time began. They called themselves "The Unitus Fratrum," or "The Unity of the Brethren," but are still affectionately known throughout the church and the world as "The Moravians." Since the apostles Peter, Paul and John, it is possible that no other three men within the same movement have so impacted the church and the world as John Huss, Jon Amos Comenius, and Count Nicolaus Ludwig von Zinzendorf. One planted the seed, one watered it, and one reaped the fruit.

War and Peace

Comenius also believed that the wars, which had brought so much tragedy into the world as well as to his own life, were the result of basic human ignorance. He began to ponder the potential of schools for providing an education for all children. This was a novel idea at the time because, outside of a few Christian and Jewish communities, education was almost exclusively limited to the children of the nobility, or merchant class, who were taught by private tutors. Comenius began to dream of schools for all children that were founded upon the truth of the gospel. He believed that the knowledge of the

Prince of Peace would be the agency for bringing peace among the nations.

Comenius determined that to accomplish his goals he had to establish quality Christian schools. To do this he would have to provide excellent curriculum material and develop effective methods of teaching that not only imparted knowledge, but stimulated a love for knowledge. He set out to find teachers who possessed above all things a deep love for God, and were of strong moral character. He especially gave himself to the training of his teachers to impart that love of God, and the reality that every child could have a close relationship with God. He gave himself with great passion to see that each child would become "a creature which shall be the joy of his creator."

In 1628, Comenius was able to establish a school in Lissa, Poland. In 1632, he was made the Bishop of the scattered Moravian brethren. As his works were published he quickly became widely known. One of his educational treatises, known as the *Janua Linguarum*, was even translated by the Moslems into Arabic, then into Turkish, Persian and Mongolian. His friends rejoiced greatly in this, believing that these translations would sow the seeds of the gospel among those nations.

Christ As All

In 1641, Comenius was invited to England by Samuel Hartlib, a friend of the renowned poet Milton. There he was persuaded to start his Pansophic College in London. Comenius' idea of pansophia was that the wisdom of God was sovereign over all things, and that all things were connected within the circle of this knowledge. He envisioned that The Pansophic

"God has His own thoughts and seasons"

College would be a place where Christian educators could gather together from Europe and America to demonstrate that there was a unity of knowledge because in Christ **"all things hold together"** (**Colossians 1:17**).

Comenius also believed that education established on this basic knowledge of Christ as the reason for all things, would bring unity to the Christian church. As Christians came into unity they would then be able to spread the gospel to all nations, which would result in the unity of all nations and the end to war. It was this idea of taking the gospel of the unity that is in Christ to all nations that would fire the heart of the young Count Zinzendorf a century later, and would give birth to modern missions.

With hopes running high just before the college was to open, the English Civil War broke out, making it impossible to proceed. Comenius again refused to be discouraged, remarking that, "God has His own thoughts and seasons." He consoled himself with the fact that the Lord would not let David build His temple, but did allow him to prepare the design and materials. Comenius then determined to continue to pursue the vision and understanding, that would one day be required by the one whom God would choose to build the college.

War and Truth

Comenius then left for Sweden where he had a major impact on the Swedish education system through his relationship with the brilliant Gustafsson Oxenstierna. In 1643, he returned to Lissa, Poland. He was then asked to be the first rector of the newly established Harvard University near Boston. He declined, deciding to stay in Lissa. There he enjoyed a few years of peace before war would again strike a tragic blow to this great man of peace. In 1656, the Catholic Poles defeated the Lutheran Swedes who had occupied much of Poland. The Catholics then condemned Lissa to be a "heretic's nest" and it was burned. Again Comenius lost all of his books and unpublished manuscripts.

Still refusing to be discouraged, Comenius became even more resolved that the truth of the gospel had to be made known, not only through the evangelistic gospel of salvation, but by planting truth in the innermost being. He saw education and the renewal of the mind by the true knowledge of Christ as the only remedy for human folly. He moved to the Netherlands where he spent the rest of his life. In spite of the almost continuous tragedies and opposition, he produced 90 books for publication. His works on education undoubtably helped to set the course of modern history. They would give new life to the whole church, and they helped engender the modern democratic movements by empowering the common people with knowledge.

Comenius believed the work of education to be the special mandate of the church, which was called to be "the light of the world." He interpreted light as true knowledge, and he believed true knowledge would always lead one to Christ, Who was the Reason for all things. He knew that only in the Prince of Peace would the world ever come to know true peace.

"Those who trust their lives to the grace of God, regardless of persecutions or problems, are always used as the vessels of resurrection power."

Like his Savior, the great apostle Paul, and multitudes of faithful since, Comenius died nearly alone, and without being able to personally witness very much fruit from his great labors. But he had faith, **"the assurance of things hoped for, the conviction of things not seen" (Hebrews 11:1).** Like the great heros of the faith before him, he remained a stranger and an exile on earth. He was a citizen of "another country," and never lost his vision for **"the city which has foundations, whose architect and builder is God" (verse 10).** For these God has prepared a city, because they **"endured as seeing Him who is unseen" (verse 27).**

Through Tribulation He Entered the Kingdom

Satan had thought that the best way to deal with Jesus was to crucify Him. That plan backfired to his own destruction. He obviously thought that the best way to deal with Comenius was with wars, tragedies and the constant destruction of his work. Even so, all that the enemy meant for evil was used to plant the seeds of an even greater vision in the heart of this gentle Moravian prophet. These seeds would one day result in some of the greatest revivals in history, and some of the greatest advancements in the human condition, which is always a fruit of true revival. The Lord loves all men and desires for them to be saved. It is for that reason that He causes His sun to shine on the just and unjust, knowing that **"the kindness of God leads … to repentance" (Romans 2:4).**

Those who trust their lives to the grace of God, regardless of persecutions or problems, are always used as the vessels of resurrection power. It is the hope that we have in the resurrection that overcomes the enemy's greatest weapon against us—the fear of death. When the fear of death is conquered, all of his other yokes and devices are powerless. Those who live in the hope of the resurrection will always prevail, and not only will they prevail, they will sow in the earth seeds that cannot die.

In II Kings 13:21, we have the remarkable story of a man who was accidently cast into the grave of Elisha, as he was being buried. Though the prophet was dead, there was still so much life in his bones that when the man touched those bones, he came back to life. The bones are the framework, and sometimes we can just touch the framework of the anointed vessels of God in history and life will flow through us. The hidden seed that was first sown by John Hus, and kept alive by Comenius and Zinzendorf, is still alive. Many today who are just touching what is left of their great ministries are still being charged with resurrection power.

The Following Summarizes Comenius' Other Revolutionary Ideas on Education

☐ He was one of the first to contend for the education of women and the children of all classes of people.

☐ He promoted a varied curriculum including history, geography, science, music, singing, drama, civics and handiwork.

☐ He taught that everything in nature revealed Christ, and that *true* science would always lead to a greater knowledge of the Creator.

☐ He believed that children learned much by seeing, touching, handling and smelling, not just hearing.

☐ He taught that the school environment was crucial and that classrooms should be bright and cheerful.

☐ There were few pictures in books in the seventeenth century, so he produced a children's encyclopedia with pictures, called *Orbis Pictus*, believing that a picture could take the place of many words.

☐ According to Comenius, schools were to be "happy workshops of humanity" and "an imitation of heaven."

☐ He prescribed a considerable amount of play time in which he encouraged the teachers to participate.

☐ He taught that education was not just the acquisition of facts and knowledge, but the development of wisdom.

☐ He believed that four hours was long enough for school work, and that the day should combine both amusement and domestic duties.

☐ He felt that homework was apt to be done poorly, and that poorly done work was more hurtful than no work at all. He also opposed homework because he felt that a child's time at home could be better spent with their parents.

☐ He taught that children should learn by doing and by teaching others. Sometimes the older and more advanced children were required to instruct the younger.

☐ The children in his school were required to occasionally produce dramatic exhibitions that related to what they had been learning.

☐ He wrote that education should be "in the spring of life and in the spring of day" (the morning).

☐ He advised, "let nothing be taught which is not of the most solid utility for this life or for the next."

☐ Comenius taught that each school should produce its own trained teachers by the apprenticeship system.

☐ He taught that teachers were instruments of divine grace with a high calling, while sternly warning against professional arrogance. "Let your heavenly calling and the confidence of the parents who entrust their offspring to you be as a fire within you," he charged.

☐ The qualities he looked for in teachers included piety, diligence, paternal kindness, respect for children, the grace to accept frequent inspection, and the enthusiasm of "a miner who trembles with excitement when he discovers a rich vein of ore." ■

The photograph shows (from left to right) Rick Joyner, Leonard Jones, and John Dawson standing by the grave of Jon Amos Comenius near Amsterdam, The Netherlands.

UNITY THROUGH WORSHIP

by
JOHN HAMRICK

All Scriptures KJV.

And let us consider one another to provoke unto love and to good works: not forsaking the assembling of ourselves together, as the manner of some is; but exhorting one another: and so much the more, as ye see the day approaching (Hebrews 10:24, 25).

Then thou shalt see, and flow together, and thine heart shall fear, and be enlarged (Isaiah 60:5a).

It came even to pass, as the trumpeters and singers were as one, to make one sound to be heard in praising and thanking the Lord; and when they lifted up their voice with the trumpets and cymbals and instruments of music, and praised the Lord, saying,

For He is good; for His mercy endureth for ever: that then the house was filled with a cloud, even the house of the Lord; so that the priests could not stand to minister by reason of the cloud: for the glory of the Lord had filled the house of God (II Chronicles 5:13, 14).

And the Lord came down to see the city and the tower, which the children of men were building.

And the Lord said, Behold, the people is one, and they have all one language; and this they begin to do: and now nothing will be withheld from them, which they have imagined to do (Genesis 11:5, 6).

The Problem

An exasperated pastor once cried out, "When Satan fell from heaven, he must have fallen into the choir loft of this church." There is no more controversy to be found than that which arises over the music program of the average church. The problem lies in the words *music program*. Most of our music is programmed to please the flesh, not to lead us to the throne.

I am convinced, and I believe with scriptural support, that God built the universe on a musical foundation (see Job 38:4-7). The ability to sing, play instruments, dream, and compose music is a divine gift that should bring the strongest kind of unity and order. Instead, we have turned this divine gift into a program, set its limits, and introduced into it the seeds of disunity. God is calling the church back to the pure musical worship that will transport His people from their fleshly pursuits into His throne room, so they can make their music at His feet, for His pleasure. This cannot be programmed by mere human ingenuity.

After the fall, mankind walked in a fleshly unity that was leading them deeper into sin. So profound was their sin that God found it necessary to destroy the fleshly unity by scattering their languages (see Genesis 11:5-7). Men were using their unity to continue their rebellion by trying to get to heaven without God, and to make a name for themselves.

Since the fall God has been working with His creation to restore true spiritual unity to the end that it will lead us back into the intimacy with Him that was lost by the fall. Part of that restoration is through the corporate Body of Christ, the church. One of God's gifts to the church for this unity is music. The aim of our assembling together is that we would establish a common flow that will lead us to the throne. Flow is the operative word. We are charged with helping each other flow together from where we are to a place of true worship before the throne of God.

When we meet together we are normally at some level of our fleshly existence. We may be up or down, depending on what has been happening in our lives. But wherever we find ourselves on the spiritual scale, we are far short of where we want to be, and of where we *must be*—worshipping together before the throne of God. God's gift to bring us from the world of flesh to the state of worship is music. Music is a language of the spirit that transcends our minds to touch our hearts.

Flow is, admittedly, an elusive quality in our congregational worship. It is so important that we should not be content to worship without it, no matter how exciting our music program might become to the flesh.

From Darkness to Light

There is a music that is of darkness and a music that is of the light. For anyone with even basic spiritual perception pure darkness is easily distinguishable from pure light. Music, however, possesses elements of both darkness and light, and therefore each can be much more difficult to discern within this realm.

There are at least two ways to distinguish between darkness and light in music. One is to pray that God will give us discernment. We need to pray about specific forms and rhythms, and even about individual compositions.

The second way to discern light from darkness in music is to understand the destination at which we arrive as a result of the music. If we wind up in the presence of God, the music that has helped us get there is of the light. If the result is a moving away from God toward carnality, or darkness, then we can readily identify the source of that music.

This introduces an interesting paradox. The same music that brings us into the presence of God in one set of circumstances may lead us away from Him in another situation. It is a mistake to think that just because a composition stirred us toward the Lord at a certain meeting that it will always do so.

For example, Handel's composition, "The Messiah," seldom fails to stir me to seek the Master. But imagine a scene in which the church has been brought by the Spirit to a place of deep, quiet worship in which the flesh is surrendering to the realm of the Spirit. Here there is much quiet weeping as one person after another makes things right with the Lord. Then in this especially meaningful moment some well-meaning person who loves "The Messiah" as I do, turns his stereo up full blast and plays a stirring rendition of "The Hallelujah Chorus." The flow of the Spirit would almost surely be interrupted, and likely would not be recovered for a long time.

That may be a far-fetched example, but it illustrates an all-too-common experience. How many times have we been jerked away from a place of near-worship by someone who feels inspired to teach a new song? We need new songs. However, the teaching of new songs must merge with the flow of the present purposes of the Spirit or it can be counter-productive to the goal of all true ministry, which is our drawing closer to the Lord. Anyone who is to make a real contribution to the spiritual welfare of the body of Christ through music must be aware of the flow of the Spirit in the meeting. Music for music's sake can be a pleasant experience, but music for the Lord's sake must fit in with His desires and His plans.

Music as a Means of Worship

Our Lord desires that we enjoy life, and He has given us many pleasant experiences that serve no other purpose than our pleasure. Music can be such an experience. I enjoy a broad spectrum of music, including Beethoven, Glenn Miller, and Flatt and Scruggs. I don't get closer to God through such music, I just enjoy it. However, it is important that I not allow the enemy to turn my tastes to types of music that minister darkness to me, even though they may be pleasant to my flesh.

However, what concerns us here is not just pleasant sound, but spiritual experience. Call it sacred music, worship music, praise or what you will, much of it is a mixture of darkness and light; so much so that we have lost sight of what music is about in the first place.

The ultimate purpose of spiritual music is to bring us into the throne room of our Lord. We begin where we are, which is usually somewhere outside the outer court. We come to the gate filled with things of the flesh, such as personal desires, family concerns, and other worries. Each of us is encapsulated in his own world, separate and apart from all others. There is a great need in each for the praise and thanksgiving that can tear down the walls and help us move together into the presence of God.

So there is music. It is significant that we almost always begin our gatherings with music. This is because our togetherness is not togetherness until we come together in a more-than-physical sense. To be in the same room is not necessarily to experience unity. But as we join in singing we begin to flow together toward a common destination. As one of our favorite songs suggests, we forget about ourselves and concentrate on Him and worship Him.

In Satan's counterfeit, exactly the same process takes place. People gather in the relative innocence of fleshly pursuit, but the music to which they lend themselves draws them together toward a place of worship, and finally they forget about themselves and concentrate on the darkness and worship him by doing the deeds of darkness. This is why most bars and clubs feature music.

True worship is not just something we do; it is something that comes forth from us when we are in the presence of God. It is the heart-felt, and often heart-rending, expression of awe, love, healthy fear, respect, desire and other emotions that come tumbling forth when we see God. True worship is not manufactured in order to see God, but comes from having seen Him. It is what happened to Isaiah in the sixth chapter of his prophecy. It is what happened to Paul on the road to Damascus. It is what happened to Moses on Mount Sinai. And it should become our experience every time we gather in His Name, for didn't He say, "There am I in the midst of them?"

Music is only one way of worshipping God and it is an important way. But it seems that we often have gone astray by calling something that is not worship by that name.

Philosophy of Musical Worship

What is it then? I will pray with the spirit, and I will pray with the understanding also: I will sing with the spirit, and I will sing with the understanding also (I Corinthians 14:15).

Mankind is made in the image of God. The desire for music and the ability to produce it are parts of that image.

Any set of circumstances which arouses an emotion, positive or negative, eventually will bring forth a musical expression of that emotion. All music is an outpouring of man's emotional response to a set of circumstances, be they positive or negative in nature. A great military victory can bring forth an "1812 Overture." An economic depression inspires songs of worry and concern. A time of great moral turpitude such as that which we are now experiencing will bring about its own music of lasciviousness, degradation, and the base things of life.

In such cases the circumstances set the tone for the music, as an expression of the emotional reaction of the soul of man to those circumstances. Then, having received acceptance and popularity, music acts as a catalyst that helps to reproduce the circumstances from which it was born.

The music of darkness, for instance, begins as an emotional expression of the thrills of experiencing dark things. As it takes form and becomes acceptable to large segments of the population, it may become separated from its origins, but tends to promote the circumstances of those origins in its adherents.

Similarly, the music of light begins in man's experience of light, and then moves on to promote the circumstances of light in those who give themselves to it.

Thus it is important to make choices about what kind of music we allow into our lives. Since music brings with it the circumstances of its origins and plants the emotions of those origins in the souls of its adherents, we need to know from whence it comes, darkness or light.

Just as constantly absorbing pornography promotes pornographic thinking and actions, so does constantly absorbing the Word of God promote spiritual thinking and actions. Because music goes beyond the mind to the heart, it can be even more powerful than the written language. Satan carries forward his nefarious schemes by appealing to man's emotional being at every opportunity. Because of the importance of this method, he has made a specialty of distorting and misusing music for his own purposes.

In terms of the philosophy of music, then, the most important questions are: "Where is it coming from?" and "For what purpose is it presented?" If it is springing forth from a heart that is overflowing with love for God, and is presented as an offering to warm His heart, then it is true worship. Worship through music, and otherwise, can be defined as our deep emotional reaction to being in the presence of God.

It would seem axiomatic to say that not all music is Godly. Equally true, not all Godly music is the music of worship. Good music, with the right words, rhythm, melody, can serve purposes other than that of worship. Godly music can comfort, confront, encourage and strengthen. It can stir people to higher goals. It can prophesy. But ultimately, it should move us to the service and worship of our Creator.

Who Is a Musician?

Talent and training can produce a *musician*. Only the calling and anointing of God can make one a *Musician*. Pardon the play on words, but its purpose is to emphasize that God has established Musicians in the Body, even as He has established other ministries. Many can prophesy, but not many are Prophets. Many can teach, but not many are Teachers. Many can sing and play, but not many are anointed as Musicians.

Why labor with the distinction? Certainly not to lessen the contribution of anyone who is led of the Spirit to sing or play in a service. But it is important to pay close attention when one who is anointed to a particular ministry begins to move in that ministry. All worshippers, but especially those who lead in singing and playing, should subject themselves to the anointing of those whom God has selected as His Musicians. King David called them the "Chief Musicians."

I listen to all prophecy, but there are Prophets whose ministry is so tried and recognizable that I give special attention when they speak. I'll sing with anyone, but there are Musicians (Singers and Instrumentalists) whose calling and anointing is so proven and recognizable that when they begin to function I know that we are about to move closer to God. Sometimes we need to join in. Sometimes we need to listen and gather the nourishment of their ministry to our hearts.

Interestingly, although they are skilled in their calling, Musicians' qualifications lie not in their skills, but in the spiritual discernment, sensitivity and obedience within their calling. Therefore, Musicians do not have to call attention to themselves. No true Prophet has to wear an identification badge. Neither does a true Apostle, nor a true anything else in the Body. And certainly no God-called and God-anointed Musician has to be accorded the recognition of a title. The ministry will make way for itself.

We who sit under the ministry do need to have our spiritual eyes open and our hearts ready to receive when that which is anointed of God begins to function. If you are the minister, forget the recognition and just function. If you have to force recognition, it's a pretty good indication that the anointing has not yet come.

Practical Aspects of Musical Worship

There are several components of music, all of which must flow together to make a presentation both pleasing to God and up-lifting to man. These are melody, harmony, rhythm, pitch, tempo, lyrics, instruments and purpose. But the grand component, made up of all the others working together, is *flow*. Flow is almost impossible to define or describe, but it is a reality that, once experienced, becomes the object of a heart-hunger in us. We can never be content without the flow, once we have tasted it.

When there is a true flow in musical worship, one is lifted into the presence of God and is likely to forget about himself, his neighbor, and how good a job he is doing at presenting a musical offering to God. When there is true flow we tend to become the offering instead of simply presenting the offering.

How do the musical components contribute to flow? If we can find an answer to this question, we can rise above a "song service" and begin to experience true musical worship.

1. Purpose

Let's start with purpose because purpose has more to do with flow than does any other factor.

There are many valid purposes in our making of music together. One is to comfort in a time of sorrow. Another is to strengthen our weaknesses. Still another is to increase our joy. A fourth could be to set us free of inappropriate inhibitions. Another is to encourage. But we make a mistake when we lump all these together and call them "worship." In truth, none of them individually or collectively constitutes worship.

One dictionary defines worship as "reverent honor and homage paid to God." Another puts it better, I believe, when it speaks of feeling. It defines worship thus: "to feel an adoring reverence or regard for God."

Negative emotions (sorrow, fear, feelings of rejection) can certainly keep us from flowing together. But music is a powerful antidote to all these poisons. By overcoming the negatives in our lives at any given moment, music helps us come to the place where we can begin "to feel an adoring reverence or regard for God." Music used in this way may be a necessary prerequisite to true worship, but it can never replace worship!

Are we just splitting hairs? I think not, for most of our "worship" never gets past the place of ministering to the participants so that it can move on to the place of ministering to God. We need to recognize the purposes of music as valid, use them for as long as they are needed to get us beyond our selves, and then drop them behind like used booster rockets as we move into worship—a true flowing together of our hearts and the great heart of God.

So what do we need to do in a practical sense? We need to sing our good songs that help us to gain victory over the flesh, that lift us up, that strip away our fears and sorrows, that help us remember that God is truly in charge of things, and then we need to wait.

Wait! It seems the hardest thing for a group to do. But when we begin to get our attention off ourselves and on Him, then we are ready to hear from Him just what would please Him at this moment. A song, a time of quiet, a prayer of adoration, a tear, a shout, a dance—any or all of these may be what He desires of us. Presented in a spirit of "adoring reverence," these expressions will become worship in its fullest sense.

To summarize, most of us come to meetings bringing with us a potpourri of positive and negative emotions which tend to cause us to focus on ourselves and our needs. God has given us many means of meeting those needs, and one of the greatest is music. But the purpose of having our needs met is not that we have our needs met, but that we might flow together to the throne of God to worship and adore Him.

2. Instruments

God likes trumpets, cymbals, drums, harps, timbrels, psaltries, and many other instruments, including some not mentioned in the Bible like pianos and guitars. But the preeminent instrument of worship is the human voice. All other instruments are subservient to it.

There is a direct connection between the heart and the mouth. Jesus taught it pointedly in Matthew:

> ... **out of the abundance of the heart the mouth speaketh.**
>
> **A good man out of the good treasure of the heart bringeth forth good things: and an evil man out of the evil treasure bringeth forth evil things (Matthew 12:34, 35).**

The brain, the emotions, the blood, the nervous system—all of these are shared in common by all parts of the body, including the mouth and vocal cords. All instruments other than the voice produce their sounds through some mechanical or electrical means. The voice, as a part of the body, can directly express all that makes up the human being and the divine nature.

What a travesty when a mechanical voice usurps the authority of the living voice! Used to support, lift up, inspire, the mechanical or electrical is a wonderful aid. But in the time of worship, the living instrument should be given preeminence.

Often a problem arises from our tendency to equate worship and praise. Praise is essentially an offering that we lay before God. Worship is the recognition by our whole being of the infinite worth and worthiness of God.

The instrumentalists' question then becomes, "Can I not worship God on my instrument?" Of course you can! But keep in mind that we're defining worship in terms of flow. By definition, there can be no "leader" in the act of worship. Many, including singers, dancers, instrumentalists, can lead us to worship, but none can lead us in worship. If there is a leader in worship, our attention is on following the leader, not on worshipping the Lord.

Keep in mind, too, that it is almost impossible for instruments to not lead. They stand out. They command. They assert. It takes real skill and anointing to play an instrument in a group in such a way as to accompany, and not lead or drive. Few have the skill, or the anointing. The instrumentalist, then, must be particularly sensitive to the flow of the Spirit. In most cases it is the task of the instrumentalist to lead for a time, then to be led by (accompany) the primary instrument of worship, the voices.

When the time of worship comes, it takes a finely tuned sensitivity to the Spirit to know when to play and when not to play. How tempting it is to go into "ecstatic utterance" on one's instrument. It satisfies the soul of the instrumentalist like few experiences can. But the flowing together of all the human spirits and the Spirit of the Lord might actually be hindered by such "utterance."

The question again is, "Must the instrumentalist be left out of the final great outpouring to God?" And the answer again is, emphatically, "No." The instrumentalist actually has two instruments at his command—his mechanical device and his voice. The latter provides the purest expression of love he can present to his God, and it can flow together with all the other voices in a way that his mechanical device never can. He needs only the spiritual discernment to know when to lay down the one and go on to the other. The whole flow of the worship may depend upon that discernment.

3. Structure

Perhaps each element of the structure of music (melody, harmony, rhythm, pitch, tempo and lyrics) deserves its own treatise. But for our purpose, we're grouping them with only a brief paragraph or two about each.

The melody should, in most instances, be familiar, simple, pleasing to the soul, and repetitious. These are the qualities of much of the world's great music. Certainly they are the qualities that will help us come to a time of worship together. Performance skills are not the stuff of satisfying worship, or pre-worship for that matter. It is important that our souls be free to concentrate on the Lord and not be bound up in our efforts to reproduce complicated melodies.

The same is true of the rhythm. It should be simple, pleasing and uplifting. As with the melody, complicated rhythm patterns tend to claim our attention and become an end in themselves. Rhythm should be our

servant, too, and not our master. It should not overwhelm and predominate. It is a device for bringing our souls together and leading us to the Lord.

As for pitch, the important thing is that it be within comfortable reach for everyone taking part. How can this be, seeing voices differ so much? One is low, another is high. But there is a place where, if the low works to its upper limits and the high works to its lower limits, we can meet and flow with the majority who have those wonderful "in between" voices. It's just a matter of practical necessity. When you lead out in a song, pitch it where the majority will be comfortable, not where you will be comfortable. Experimentation and observation are the best teachers here.

There is a right tempo for every song. Interestingly, the same song may be right at one tempo in one meeting, and require another tempo in another meeting. Sensing the spiritual flow of the meeting is all-important in choosing the tempo. Singing too fast or too slow for the flow can be disastrous. If your spirit is at one with the Holy Spirit, you will choose the right tempo and the song will flow.

And just a word about harmony. It can be entirely within the flow of the meeting to sing harmony instead of melody. Sometimes, because of my low voice and the fact that a song may be pitched so high I can't reach the melody, I sing bass out of necessity. The only word of caution is: be sure your harmony is harmonious. A certain amount of skill and training is necessary in this special area of music, just as in the playing of instruments. But remember the principle of musical worship within which we must operate if we are worshipping: we are singing to please God, not to please ourselves.

continued on page 86

PRAYING SAINTS OF THE OLD TESTAMENT

INTERCESSION

by
E. M. BOUNDS

All Scriptures KJV.

The Holy Spirit will give to the praying saint the brightness of an immortal hope, the music of a deathless song, in His baptism and communion with the heart, He will give sweeter and more enlarged visions of heaven until the taste for other things will pall, and other visions will grow dim and distant. He will put notes of other worlds in human hearts until all earth's music is discord and songless. E.M.Bounds

Old Testament history is filled with accounts of praying saints. The leaders of Israel in those early days were noted for their praying habits. Prayer is the one thing which stands out prominently in their lives.

To begin with, note the incident in Joshua, 10th chapter, where the very heavenly bodies were made subject to prayer. A prolonged battle was on between the Israelites and their enemies, and when night was rapidly coming on, and it was discovered that a few more hours of daylight were needful to ensure victory for the Lord's hosts, Joshua, that sturdy man of God, stepped into the breach, with prayer. The sun was too rapidly declining in the west for God's people to reap the full fruits of a noted victory, and Joshua, seeing how much depended upon the occasion, cried out in the sight and in the hearing of Israel, **"Sun, stand thou still upon Gibeon; and thou, Moon, in the Valley of Ajalon."** The sun actually stood still and the moon stopped on her course at the command of this praying man of God, till the Lord's people had avenged themselves upon the Lord's enemies.

Jacob was not a strict pattern of righteousness, prior to his all-night praying. Yet he was a man of prayer and believed in the God of prayer. So we find him swift to call upon God in prayer when he was in trouble. He was fleeing from home fearing Esau, on his way to the home of Laban, a kinsman. As night came, he lighted on a certain place to refresh himself with sleep, and as he slept he had a wonderful dream in which he saw the angels of God ascending and descending on a ladder which stretched from earth to heaven. It was no wonder when he awoke he was constrained to exclaim, **"Surely the Lord is in this place; and I knew it not."**

Then he entered into a very definite covenant with Almighty God, and in prayer vowed a vow unto the Lord, saying:

If God will be with me, and will keep me in this way that I go, and will give me bread to eat and raiment to put on, so that I come again to my father's house in peace; then shall the Lord be my God: and this stone, which I have set for a pillar, shall be God's house: and of all that thou shalt give me, I will surely give the tenth unto thee.

With a deep sense of his utter dependence upon God, and desiring above all the help of God, Jacob conditioned his prayer for protection, blessing and guidance by a solemn vow. Thus Jacob supported his prayer to God by a vow.

Twenty years had passed while Jacob tarried at the house of Laban, and he had married two of his daughters and God had given him children. He had increased largely in wealth, and he resolved to leave that place and return home to where he had been reared. Nearing home it occurred to him that he must meet his brother Esau, whose anger had not abated notwithstanding the passage of many years. God, however, had said to him, **"Return unto the land of thy father, and to thy kindred, and I will be with thee."** In this dire emergency doubtless God's promise and his vow made long ago came to his mind,

and he took himself to an all-night season of prayer.

Here comes to our notice that strange, inexplicable incident of the angel struggling with Jacob all night long, till Jacob at last obtained the victory. **"I will not let thee go, except thou bless me."** And then and there, in answer to his earnest, pressing and importunate praying, he was richly blessed personally and his name was changed. But even more than that, God went ahead of Jacob's desire, and strangely moved upon the angry nature of Esau, and lo and behold, when Jacob met him the next day, Esau's anger had entirely abated, and he vied with Jacob in showing kindness to his brother who had wronged him. No explanation of this remarkable change in the heart of Esau is satisfactory which leaves out prayer.

Samuel, the mighty intercessor in Israel and a man of God, was the product of his mother's prayer. Hannah is a memorable example of the nature and benefits of importunate praying. No son had been born to her and she yearned for a man child. Her whole soul was in her desire. So she went to the house of worship, where Eli, the priest of God, was, and staggering under the weight of that which bore down on her heart she was beside herself and seemed to be really intoxicated. Her desires were too intense for articulation. **"She poured out her soul in prayer before the Lord."** Insuperable natural difficulties were in the way, but she "multiplied her praying," as the passage means, till her God-lightened heart and her bright face recorded the answer to her prayers, and Samuel was hers by a conscious faith and a nation was restored by faith.

Samuel was born in answer to the vowful prayer of Hannah, for the solemn covenant which she made with God if He would grant her request must not be left out of the account in investigating this incident of a praying woman and the answer she received. It is suggestive in James 5:15 that **"The *prayer* of faith shall save the sick,"** the word translated prayer, means *a vow*. So that prayer in its highest form of faith is that prayer which carries the whole man as a sacrificial offering. Thus devoting the whole man himself, and his all, to God in a definite, intelligent vow, never to be broken, in a quenchless and impassioned desire to heaven—such an attitude of self-devotement to God mightily helps praying.

Samson is somewhat of a paradox when we examine his religious character. But amid all his faults, which were grave in the extreme, he knew the God who hears a prayer and he knew how to talk to God.

No farness to which Israel had gone, no depth to which Israel had fallen, no chains however iron with which Israel was bound but that their cry to God easily spanned the distance, fathomed the depths, and broke the chains. It was the lesson they were ever learning and always forgetting, that prayer always brought God to their deliverance, and that there was nothing too hard for God to do for His people. We find all of God's saints at different times in some way or another, in such a place. Their straits are, however, often the heralds of their great triumphs. But for whatever cause their straits come, or of what kind soever, there is no strait of any degree of direness or from any source whatsoever of any nature whatsoever, from which prayer could not extricate them. The great strength of Samson does not relieve him nor extricate him out of his straits. Read what the Scriptures say:

And when he came unto Lehi, the Philistines shouted against him; and the Spirit of the Lord came mightily upon him: and the cords that were upon his arms became as flax that was burnt with fire, and his bands loosed from off his hands.

And he found a new jawbone of an ass, and put forth his hand, and took it, and slew a thousand men therewith.

And Samson said, With the jawbone of an ass, heaps upon heaps, with the jaw of an ass have I slain a thousand men.

And it came to pass, when he had made an end of speaking, that he cast away the jawbone out of his hand, and called that place Ramath-lehi.

And he was sore athirst, and called on the Lord, and said, Thou hast given this great deliverance into the hand of thy servant: and now shall I die for thirst, and fall into the hand of the uncircumcised?

But God clave a hollow place that was in the jaw, and there came water thereout; and when he had drunk, his spirit came again, and he revived (Judges 15:14-19).

We have another incident in the case of this strange Old Testament character, showing how, when in great straits, these saints' minds involuntarily turned to God in prayer. However irregular in life they were, however far from God they departed, however sinful they might be when trouble came upon these men, they invariably called upon God for deliverance, and, as a rule, when they repented God heard their cries and granted their requests. This incident comes at the close of Samson's life, and shows us how his life ended.

Read the record as found in Judges, 16th chapter. Samson had formed an alliance with Delilah, a heathen woman, and she, in connivance with the Philistines, sought to discover the source of his immense strength. Three successive times she failed, and at last by her persistence and womanly arts persuaded Samson to divulge to her the wonderful secret. So in an unsuspecting hour he disclosed to her the fact that the source of his strength was in his hair which had never been cut; and she deprived him of his great physical power by cutting off his hair. She called for the Philistines, and they came and put out his eyes and otherwise mistreated him.

On an occasion when the Philistines were gathered to offer a great sacrifice to Dagon, their idol god, they called for Samson to make sport for them. And the following is the account as he stood there, presumably the laughing-stock of these enemies of his and of God.

And Samson said unto the lad that held him by the hand, Suffer me that I may feel the pillars whereupon the house standeth, that I may lean upon them.

Now the house was full of men and women; and all the lords of the Philistines were there; and there were upon the roof about three thousand men and women, that beheld while Samson made sport.

And Samson called unto the Lord, and said, O Lord God, remember me, I pray thee, and strengthen me, I pray thee, only this once, O God, that I may be at once avenged of the Philistines for my two eyes. And Samson took hold of the two middle pillars upon which the house stood, and on which it was borne up, of the one with his right hand; and of the other with his left.

And Samson said, Let me die with the Philistines. And he bowed himself with all his might; and the house fell upon the lords, and upon all the people that were therein. So the dead which he slew at his death were more than they which he slew in his life (Judges 16:26-30).

Jonah, the man who prayed in the fish's belly, brings to view another remarkable instance of these Old Testament worthies who were given to prayer. This man Jonah, a prophet of the Lord, was a fugitive from God and from the place of duty. He had been sent on a mission of warning to wicked Nineveh, and had been commanded to cry out against them, **"for their wickedness is come up before me,"** said God. But Jonah, through fear or otherwise, declined to obey God, and took passage on a ship for Tarshish, fleeing from God. He seems to have overlooked the plain fact that the same God who had sent him on that alarming mission had His eye upon him as he hid himself on board that vessel. A storm arose as the vessel was on its way to Tarshish, and it was decided to throw Jonah overboard in order to appease God and to avert the destruction of the boat and of all on board. But God was there as He had been with Jonah from the beginning. He had prepared a great fish to swallow

Jonah, in order to arrest him, to defeat him in his flight from the post of duty, and to save Jonah that he might help to carry out the purposes of God.

It was Jonah who was in the fish's belly, in that great strait, and passing through a strange experience, who called upon God, who heard him and caused the fish to vomit him out on dry land. What possible force could rescue him from this fearful place? He seemed hopelessly lost, in "the belly of hell," as good as dead and damned. But he prays—what else can he do? And this is just what he had been accustomed to do when in trouble before.

I cried by reason of mine affliction unto the Lord, and he heard me; out of the belly of hell cried I, and thou heardest my voice.

And the Lord spake unto the fish, and it vomited out Jonah upon the dry land.

Like others he joined prayer to a vow he had made, for he says in his prayer, **"But I will sacrifice unto thee with the voice of thanksgiving; I will pay that I have vowed. Salvation is of the Lord."**

Prayer was the mighty force which brought Jonah from "the belly of hell." Prayer, mighty prayer, has secured the end. Prayer brought God to the rescue of unfaithful Jonah, despite his sin of fleeing from duty, and God could not deny his prayer. Nothing is too hard for prayer because nothing is too hard for God.

That answered prayer of Jonah in the fish's belly in its mighty results became an Old Testament type of the miraculous power displayed in the resurrection of Jesus Christ from the dead. Our Lord puts His seal of truth upon the fact of Jonah's prayer and resurrection.

Nothing can be simpler than these cases of God's mighty deliverance. Nothing is plainer than that prayer has to do with God directly and simply. Nothing is clearer than that prayer has its own worth and significance in the great fact that God hears and answers prayer. This the Old Testament saints strongly believed. It is the one fact that stands out continuously and prominently in their lives. They were essentially men of prayer.

How greatly we need a school to teach the art of praying! This simplest of all arts and mightiest of all forces is ever in danger of being forgotten or depraved. The further we get away from our mother's knees, the further do we get away from the true art of praying. All our after-schooling and our after-teachers unteach us the lessons of prayer. Men prayed well in Old Testament times because they were simple men and lived in simple times. They were childlike, lived in childlike times and had childlike faith.

In citing the Old Testament saints noted for their praying habits, by no means must David be overlooked, a man who preeminently was a man of prayer. With him prayer was a habit, for we hear him say, **"Evening and morning and at noon will I pray and cry aloud."** Prayer with the Sweet Psalmist of Israel was no strange occupation. He knew the way to God and was often found in that way. It is no wonder we hear his call so clear and impressive, **"O come, let us worship and bow down; let us kneel before the Lord our maker."** He knew God as the one being who could answer prayer: **"O thou that hearest prayer, unto thee shall all flesh come."**

When God smote the child born of Bathsheba, because David had by his grievous sins given occasion of the enemies of God to blaspheme, it is no surprise that we find him engaged in a week's praying, asking God for the life of the child. The habit of his life asserted itself in this great emergency in his home, and we find him fasting and praying for the child to recover. The fact that God denied his request does not at all affect the question of David's habit of praying. Even though he did not receive what he asked for, his faith in God was not in the least affected. The fact is that while God did not give him the life of that baby boy, He afterward gave him another son, even Solomon. So that possibly the latter son was a far greater blessing to him than would have been the child for whom he prayed.

In close connection with this season of prayer, we must not overlook David's penitential praying when Nathan, by command of God, uncovered David's two great sins of adultery and murder. At once David acknowledged his wickedness, saying unto Nathan, **"I have sinned."** And as showing his deep grief over his sin, his heart-broken spirit, and his genuine repentance, it is only necessary to read Psalm 51 where confession of sin, deep humiliation and prayer are the chief ingredients of the psalm.

David knew where to find a sin-pardoning God, and was received back again and had the joys of salvation restored to him by earnest, sincere, penitential praying. Thus are all sinners brought into the divine favor, thus do they find pardon, and thus do they find a new heart. The entire Book of Psalms brings prayer to the front, and prayer fairly bristles before our eyes as we read this devotional book of the Scriptures.

Nor must even Solomon be overlooked in the famous catalogue of men who prayed in Old Testament times. Whatever their faults, they did not forget the God who hears prayer nor did they cease to seek the God of prayer. While this wise man in his later life departed from God, and his sun set under a cloud, we find him praying at the commencement of his reign.

Solomon went to Gibeon to offer sacrifice, which always meant that prayer went in close companionship with sacrifice, and while there, the Lord appeared to Solomon in a vision by night, saying unto him, "Ask what I shall give thee." The sequel shows the material out of which Solomon's character was formed. What was his request?

O Lord my God, thou hast made thy servant king instead of David my father: and I am but a little child: I know not how to go out or to come in.

And thy servant is in the midst of thy people which thou hast chosen, a great people, that cannot be numbered nor counted for multitude.

Give therefore thy servant an understanding heart to judge thy people, that I may discern between good and bad: for who is able to judge this thy so great a people? (I Kings 3:7-9).

We do not wonder that it is recorded as a result of such praying:

And the speech pleased the Lord, that Solomon had asked this thing.

And God said unto him, Because thou hast asked this thing, and hast not asked for thyself long life; neither hast asked riches for thyself, nor hast asked the life of thy

enemies; but hast asked for thyself understanding to discern judgment;

Behold I have done according to thy words: lo, I have given thee a wise and an understanding heart; so that there was none like thee before thee, neither after thee shall any arise like unto thee.

Also I have given thee that which thou hast not asked, both riches, and honour; so that there shall not be any among the kings like unto thee all thy days (I Kings 3:10-13).

What praying was this! What self-deprecation and simplicity! "I am but a little child." How he specified the one thing needful! And see how much more he received than that for which he asked!

Take the remarkable prayer at the dedication of the temple. Possibly this is the longest recorded prayer in God's Word. How comprehensive, pointed, intensive, it is! Solomon could not afford to lay the foundations of God's house in anything else but in prayer. And God heard this prayer as he heard him before, **"Now when Solomon had made an end of praying, the fire came down from heaven, and consumed the burnt offering and the sacrifices; and the glory of the Lord filled the house,"** thus God attested the acceptance of this house of worship and of Solomon, the praying king.

The list of these Old Testament saints given to prayer grows as we proceed, and is too long to notice at length all of them. But the name of Isaiah, the great evangelical prophet, must not be left out of the account. Still others might be mentioned. These are sufficient, and with their names we may close the list. Let careful readers of the Old Testament Scriptures keep the prayer question in mind, and they will see how great a place prayer occupied in the minds and lives of the men of those early days. ■

E. M. Bounds was a chaplin in the confederate Army during the Civil War. Later he wrote a series of books on prayer that are considered by many to be the best ever written on the subject. You may order all of these books in one volume from MorningStar Publications, 16000 Lancaster Hwy, Charlotte, NC 28277, Phone: (704)542-0278 or FAX (704)542-0280.

✣ Mustard Seeds of Wisdom

"It seems to me we are advertising and advocating a Christianity that has the color, but not the character of the real thing. Anything in the spiritual life that savors of discipline or of really 'taking up the cross' is termed legalism and is despised; on the other hand, what some call liberty is but self-granted license"

— *Leonard Ravenhill*

JEALOUSY, OUR HIDDEN SIN continued from page 27

Just like you, I have had my struggles with jealousy. My only hope is Jesus. His strength is perfected in me when I daily acknowledge my weakness. He is everything that I am not; the most secure, successful Being in the universe, and He dwells within me. What a wonderful testimony we have in the apostle Paul's statement **"It is no longer I who live but Christ lives in me"** (Galatians 2:20).

Responding to Jealousy

How do we respond wisely to jealousy in others? That's a whole new subject, but let me give you these five suggestions.

1. *Don't provoke jealousy through unwise communications.* **"Let us not become boastful, challenging one another, envying one another"** (Galatians 5:26).

2. *Minister grace to others by declaring their value to you and your need of them.*

3. *Withdraw from a person demonstrating* *open hatred or destructive manipulation.* The Bible says, **"… avoid such men as these"** (see II Timothy 3:1-5).

4. *Do not fear men.* Psalm 27:1 says, **"The Lord is the defense of my life; whom shall I dread?"**

5. *Bless those that curse you.* Pray down every blessing on those who through insecurity and pride have stumbled in their relationship with us and are manifesting the marks of jealousy. ■

"Jealousy" was reprinted from an article in The Last Days Magazine, a colorfully illustrated publication filled with challenging articles, ministry opportunities, and more! If you would like to receive a gift of six issues, send your request to: Last Days Ministries, Box 40, Lindale, TX 75771-0040. For additional copies of this article order LD#78. This teaching is also available on audio and video cassettes. For a listing of all tracts, audio and video teachings, and the music of Keith Green and Bob Ayala all available at whatever you can afford request our free Ministry Materials Catalogue. Pretty Good Printing, @1985 Last Day, Ministries. All Rights Reserved 2-89 (Used by permission)

A PROPHETIC LESSON continued from page 53

during those times of inactivity when God shows us His ways and prepares us for His activity, which will certainly follow. God is never late; He is always on time. The prophet Isaiah said, **"For since the beginning of the world men have not heard nor perceived by the ear, Nor has the eye seen any God besides You, who acts for the one who waits for Him"** (Isaiah 64:4).

I believe that there will be times when God's people will come upon genuine accident scenes—many far worse than what I've described—and the dead will be raised. The key to raising the dead is knowing the One who is the Resurrection and the Life. Jesus is God's agenda. When He is truly lifted up we will be allowed to do things that draw men, because they will not be drawn to us or to the acts, but to Him. When God's agenda, the glorification of His Son, becomes our agenda, the miraculous will occur. ■

David White is pastor of Calvary Baptist Church in Columbia , Mississippi, and travels widely as a teacher and evangelist. For more information about his ministry you may contact the MorningStar offices.

JUDGING PROPHECY continued from page 57

All over the world, men and women are actually hearing from the Lord about similar things, but are unable to clearly communicate them to us. There is an unwillingness to hear such things because they do not line up with what some brethren have dictated concerning the endtimes. When England was pressed against the wall during World War II, Churchill formed a plan for the liberating of Europe from the Nazis. Though things looked grim for England, his eyes were on the vision. His practical plans and those of his allies resulted in the defeat of the Nazis.

We need to stop looking for a quick way out. We need to concentrate on plans to live victoriously through the difficulties the future may hold. What if we make long range plans and Jesus returns before they are completed? No problem! We will not have wasted our time and resources in His eyes. We will gain His commendation, not His criticism. We will have been busy about the Master's business and He will be pleased. ■

Originally from England, Keith A Hazell and his wife Nova reside in Lethbridge, Alberta, Canada. He serves as part of the Leadership team of New Hope Christian Center from where he gives oversight to some 40 churches in Life-Links International Fellowship. He also travels extensively and teaches in "Schools of the Prophets." He can be reached by writing: Global Impact Ministries 4101, 20th Avenue South, Lethbridge AB, Canada, T1K 4X8.

UNITY THROUGH WORSHIP continued from page 77

In Conclusion

Interestingly, when we sing the songs we know and love, whether they be scripture songs (some call them choruses, but that is a misnomer), hymns, anthems or whatever, we each sing the *same melody,* to the *same* beat, in the *same pitch.* If any participant varies from these in any major way it brings confusion to the whole service.

In contrast, when we sing "in the Spirit" each sings *his own melody,* at his *own tempo,* in his *own pitch,* with his *own lyrics,* and yet there is no more beautiful sound than that of hundreds voices lifted up to God in this manner. Only the Spirit of God can bring about such beauty out of what should be chaos. And unless the Holy Spirit is leading it, chaos is exactly what we get.

So let this simple teaching conclude with an exhortation. Because music is a gift of God given for the special purpose of bringing us together in our spirits, and then into union with the Spirit of God, let us approach every song we sing as a spiritual experience. Let us give as much prayerful attention to the leading of the Holy Spirit in the selection, the pitch, the tempo of each song as we would in a potential major change in our life situation. Then we will worship together in Spirit and in Truth. ■

John Hamrick has been in full-time ministry for over 40 years. He continues to serve in an itinerant teaching ministry throughout the United States. He and his wife, Martha, have been married 47 years. They have 3 sons and live in Powder Springs, GA.

Remember the Titanic?
Pride and Apathy Caused the Problem ...
Preparedness is the Solution!

" IN THE NEAR FUTURE devastating economic problems will be sweeping the world like waves. Like the passengers of the Titanic, the water will lap around our ankles, then our knees, then there will be a mad rush to the highest part of the ship. But we don't have to go down with the ship, because we don't have to be on it.

STEPS OF PREPARATION must be taken immediately to prepare ourselves, our families and our friends so that we, like the courageous Captain Rostran and the crew of the Carpanthia, can offer help, both physically and spiritually. "

—Rick Joyner
THE HARVEST

ECONOMICS 101

Economics is refered to as "a window into the soul." What can be seen through this window today? **Pure monetary mythology.**

Consider just the visible tip of the iceberg: spiraling debt (soon followed by hyper-inflation), devaluing currency, and record high bankruptcies. But what's the root cause? Disobedience to God's Word.

In fact, noted Christian economist R.E. McMaster Jr., refers to our modern paper money system as "occultic!" Monetary plunder has become a way of life during the 20th century. Yet many are unaware that the U.S. economy is rapidly taking water, much like the Titanic, and are woefully **unprepared!**

The watertight monetary foundation found in scripture—gold and silver coin (also mandated in our Constitution)—has withstood the test of time. It might become your *only* financial lifeboat—*soon!*

ECONOMIC SOLUTIONS

For too long Christians have remained apathetic regarding the *true* problems with our economy. The time has come to learn from history—to understand *why* every paper money system always falls to its true value ... *zero!*

Swiss America, a major gold, silver, and certified rare coin firm, wants to help you understand the economic realities—so you can be prepared! They have just published a new book entitled, "ECONOMIC SOLUTIONS." It will explain the Federal Reserve banking system (a private Corporation!), why they create inflation-recession cycles —and what you can do to protect your hard *earned* assets with hard *owned* assets.

Also, it will help you sort out the so-called "new world order" agenda from a Biblical worldview.

Call today to find out how you can receive your copy ... FREE!

(800) 289-2646

Living Water Journal

Each quarterly edition of the *Living Water* Journal is an in-depth topical study of a principle from the kingdom of God designed to enlighten and challenge the believer.

🦢 🦢 🦢

One Year Subscription - 4 Issues
$9.00 U.S.   **$14.00** Int'l

Name_____
Address_____
City_____
State_____ Zip_____

Please make checks payable and mail to:
***Living Water* Publications**
P.O. Box 4653
Rockford, IL 61110

The man on the right has read
the book <u>Intimacy With God.</u>
The man on the left hasn't. Poor guy.

At last, an easy to understand book on how to Walk In The Spirit Continuously. Unsolicited letters claim it's the best manual for teaching young Christians. **111 pages, 36 illustrations by Patrick McIntyre**
call 1-800-598-0584 $5.95 + $1.95 S&H

GRACE TRAINING CENTER
of Kansas City
(A MINISTRY OF METRO VINEYARD FELLOWSHIP)

Sam Storms, Ph.D.
PRESIDENT

*Grace Training Center is committed to both the **centrality of Scripture** and the **power of the Holy Spirit** in the context of the local church. Our goal is **to equip** men and women for service in God's kingdom by nurturing a biblical harmony between **theological integrity** and **Spirit-empowered passion for Jesus**.*

Mike Bickle
DIRECTOR

FACULTY
◆ Sam Storms, Ph.D.
◆ Wes Adams, Ph.D.
◆ Mike Bickle
◆ Michael Kailus, M.Div.
◆ Philip Pidgeon, D.Min.
◆ Jim Goll, B.S.
◆ Noel Alexander, M.Div.
◆ Rob Black, M.A.
◆ Avner Boskey, Th.M.
◆ Tim Gustafson, M.Div.
◆ Bruce McGregor, M.Div.

- **In-depth Biblical Studies**
- **Cultivating Holy Passion For God**
- **Ministry In The Power Of The Spirit**
- **Nurture Of Prophetic Ministry**
- **Intercession For Revival**
- **Worship And The Arts**
- **Leadership Development**
- **Training In Godly Character**
- **Cell Group Based Ministry**
- **Missions & Church Planting Vision**

◆ **1, 2, and 3 Year Study Programs**
◆◆ **Internship Program**
◆◆◆ **Low Tuition Costs**

For a free brochure and more information, call or write
GRACE TRAINING CENTER
11610 Grandview Rd.
Kansas City, MO 64137
Ph: (816) 765-4282 Fax: (816) 767-1455

The Morning Star Journal is dedicated to promoting interchange between different streams, emphases, and denominations in the Body of Christ. One such way that we pursue this is to provide an opportunity for churches, ministries, and Christian businesses to advertise their goods and services.

In The Morning Star Journal **Advertising section,** we offer space for ads from 1/4 page to a full page in size. We can accept a formatted layout or design one for you.

*Orders for advertising space in the journal must be placed one quarter (minimum) prior to the distribution of the issue(s) in which you wish the advertisement to appear.

For more **information** contact:

> The Morning Star Journal
> Attention: Managing Editor
> 16000 Lancaster Hwy.
> Charlotte, NC 28277 -2061
> (704) 542-0278 - Phone

◆ JOURNAL ◆ The Morning Star

ADVERTISING OPPORTUNITIES

ORDERING

...FOR MORNINGSTAR PRODUCTS FEATURED IN THIS JOURNAL—

3 EASY WAYS TO ORDER:

1 - PHONE (704) 542-0278   (credit card or COD orders)

or 1-800-542-0278 **(Orders only)**

2 - FAX (704) 542-0280   (credit card or COD orders)

3 - MAIL ORDER TO: (must include full payment)

MORNINGSTAR PUBLICATIONS
16000 LANCASTER HWY.
CHARLOTTE, NC 28277-2061

SHIPPING:	U.S.	FOREIGN
Orders < $10.00	$2.00	$3.00
$10.00 - $24.99	$3.00	$5.50
$25.00 - $49.99	$4.00	$8.00
$50.00 - &74.99	$5.00	$10.00
$75.00 - $99.99	$6.00	$13.00
> $100.00	FREE!	FREE!

CREDIT CARD ORDERS MAY BE PHONED OR FAXED

MorningStar
PUBLICATIONS

VISA ACCEPTED **MasterCard**

Business listings in this section are not necessarily endorsements by MorningStar Publications, the authors, or the editors.

ACCOUNTING SERVICES

Barbara M. Holmes CPA, CFP
Certified Public Accountant
and Certified Financial Planner
420 Middle Highway
Barrington, RI 02806
(401) 247-2634
(401) 247-0787

BOOKS/PERIODICALS

Books
"The Destiny Of America:
A Prophetic Warning to the U.S.A."
Expanded Edition. Now is the
Time! by Timothy G. Snodgrass
Write: TGS, P. O. Box 1242
Bend, OR 97709
Enclose $7.95 plus $1.05 P&H.
Make checks out to: TGS.

Periodicals
Prophetic Ministries Canada
Canadian Newsletter/$10 yr.
66080 - 29 Ave NE
Calgary, AB
Canada T1Y 3W5
(403) 293-7150
(403) 280-6894 FAX

BUSINESS OPPORTUNITIES

Consulting With Confidence
(Behavioral & Career Consulting
Program)
Jane Roqueplot, Program Director
The Institute for Motivational
Living, Inc.
3307 Wilmington Rd.
New Castle, PA 16105
(800) 779-3472
(412) 658-7310 (FAX)

BUSINESS SERVICES

Electronic Banking Services
Serving Merchants and Ministries
Bankcard Merchant Accounts,
Check Guarantee, Phone/Fax
Checks
Mail/Phone Order Merchants OK!
(404) 565-9942

CHURCHES

Northeast
Cape Cod Christian Center
Tom Dobrient, Pastor
Meeting in the Holiday Inn
Rt. 132
Hyannis, MA 02601
(508) 771-0244

Gateway Christian Fellowship
Brian Simmons, Pastor
870 First Ave.
West Haven, CT 06516
(203) 934-0880

Joyful Noise Community
(House Church)
Kent McCuen
22 Harding Ave.
Hatboro, PA 19040
(215) 675-6134
Northern Suburbs of Philadelphia

New Life Christian Fellowship
Steve Bunkoff, Ralph Diaz, Pastors
Route 32, P.O. Box 217
Vails Gate, NY 12584
(914) 534-3077

Victory Ministries
Dr. Omar & Ilona Mednis, Pastors
3125 Rt. 10 East
Denville, NJ 07834
(201) 328-4477
(201) 267-1444

South
Calvary Baptist Church
David White, Pastor
1309 Church St.
Columbia, MS 39429
(601) 736-6336

Conerstone Christian Center
Ken Bradley, Pastor
457 Hwy 72, P.O. Box 805
Collierville, TN 38027-0805
(901) 756-4488

East Texas Christian Fellowship
Burton McDonald, Pastor
P.O. Box 707
Kirbyville, TX 75956
(409) 423-4771
(409) 423-5159 (FAX)

Fellowship of Zion
John S. Cooper, Pastor
2979 Big Texas Valley Road
Rome, GA 30165
(706) 232-4309

Greenhouse Community Church
Philip Lykes & Dave Baker,
Pastors
2023 Pipkin Rd. W.
(Mail: P.O. Box 6203)
Lakeland, FL 33807-6203
(813) 647-9706

James Avenue Baptist Church
5745 James Avenue
Fort Worth, TX 76134
(817) 293-5050

Jubilee Fellowship
Dale Moore, Pastor
P.O. Box 849221
Pembroke Pines, FL 33084
(305) 435-5341, voice
(305) 435-2793 (FAX)
E-mail, AmericaOnline
(Phntmfngrs)

Riverside Christian Fellowship
Steven Witt, Pastor
3301 Riverside Drive
Coral Springs, FL 33065

The Missionary Church International
(A Convention of Churches)
Benjamin H. Covington, Bishop
P.O. Box 1761
Columbia, SC 29202
(803) 799-0502
(803) 254-7446 (FAX)

Midwest
Vineyard Christian Fellowship of Logansport
Bruce Vernon, Pastor
One block west of Co. Rd. 600 E and 250 S
Logansport, IN 46947
(219) 753-7364

The King's House
Al Keech, Pastor
P.O. Box 612
Naperville, IL 60566
(708) 355-1955
(708) 668-9448 (FAX)

Outside US
Abundant Life Christian Fellowship
John Woods, Senior Pastor
3G Crestlea Crescent
Nepean, Ontario
Canada K2G 4N1
(613) 228-1796

CHURCH NETWORKS

The Missionary Church International
(with IRS Group Exemption Status)
Benjamin H. Covington, Bishop
P.O. Box 1761
Columbia, SC 29202
(803) 799-0502
(803) 254-7446 (FAX)

COMMUNITY

The Gathering Place
A ministering farm community
Bob Bone
P.O. Box 1365
Blountsville, AL 35031
(205) 466-5126

COMPUTERS

Bible Software
Bible Works for Windows & Mac
Hermeneutika
Mark Rice
P.O. Box 98563
Seattle, WA 98198-0563
(206) 824-WORD (9763)
(206) 824-7160 (FAX)

COUNSELING

Lovingkindness Counseling
Carey & Suzanne Ramsey
P.O. Box 176
1490 National Hwy.
Thomasville, NC 27360
(910) 886-1276

Restoration Life Ministries
Ray Kiertekles
6045 Barfield Rd, Suite 119
Atlanta, GA 30328
(404) 252-4656

Marriage/Family
Shepherd's Heart, Inc.
Dr. Harold & Ann Hammond
10516 Acacia Lane
Fairfax, VA 22032
(703) 323-6212

Psychotherapy
Dr. Sandra Joy K. Bowen
8303 Arlington Blvd., Suite 210
Fairfax, VA 22031
(703) 573-9186

Professional Christian Counseling Services
William Vaughters, MSW
228 Northwest B
Grants Pass, OR 97526
(503) 474-3524

FINANCIAL SERVICES

Financial Counseling/ Brokerage
Jay Cunningham
A.G. Edwards & Sons, Inc.
1350 W Lake Street
Roselle, IL 60172
(708) 980-7300
(800) 843-3542

Investment Advisors

Carolina Investment Advisors
R. Graham Pitt
P.O. Box 112
Shelby, NC 28150
(704) 481-0101

HEALTH, NUTRITION AND FITNESS

Kalo Vita
"The Good Life Company"
is endorsed by Pat Robertson.
Indep. Rep.: Paul Jablonowski
For a free information package,
call (205) 883-9193

HEATING & AIR CONDITIONING

Cunningham Air and Heat
Greg Cunningham, Owner
117 Boles
Osceola, IN 46561
(219) 674-6991

INSURANCE

Term Insurance
Jim D. Yarbrough, CLU, ChFC
Chartered Financial Consultant
8344 E. R.L. Thornton Exp., #400
Dallas, TX 75228
(800) 369-8132
(214) 328-5458

JEWELERS

New Beginnings by Drake Drake & Son Manufacturing Jewelers
Darlon & Glenda Drake
119 N. Texas St., P.O. Box 514
Emory, TX 75440
(903) 473-8080

LODGING

"Elegant Country Inn Lodging"
The Seal Beach Inn & Gardens
212 5th St.
Seal Beach, CA 90740
Call 1-800- HIDEAWAY

MINISTRIES

Praise Alive Ministries
Evangelist/Psalmist
Roger and Arlene Reeder
P.O. Box 1391
Jasper, AL 35502-1391
(205) 483-0800

Evangelists
Philadelphia Area
Coalition of Evangelists
"Equipping & Mobilization"
22 Harding Ave
Hatboro, PA 19040
(215) 675-6134

Evangelist/
Prophetic Ministry
Voice to the Nations
Beatrice Joan Schmitz, Pres.
P.O. Box 1571
Lakeland, FL 33802-1571
(813) 688-0850 Phone & Fax

Evangelist/
Prophetic Teaching
Eric Sigman
1114 Pine Valley Road
Griffin, GA 30223-4953
(404) 227-0937

Prison Ministry
Souls Outreach Ministries
Dr. Wocloy Choplin
900 Weeks Road
Cleveland, TN 37312-5533
(615) 479-2778

Prophetic Ministry
David Roch Growth Ministries
Newsletter, Canadian
66080 - 29 Ave NE
Calgary, AB
Canada T1Y 3W5
(403) 293-7150
(403) 280-6894 FAX

Fatherpower Ministries, Inc.
Don and Kay Wood
P.O. Box 91026
Lakeland, FL 33804
(813) 853-8769

Michael Robinson Ministries
5400 Yorkshire Street
Springfield, VA 22151-1202
(703) 978-2270

The Sower, Inc.
Burton "Bud" McDonald
P.O. Box 922
Kirbyville, TX 75956
(409) 423-4771
(409) 423-5159 (FAX)

Victory Ministries
School of the Prophets
Ilona Mednis, Pastor
3125 Route 10 East
Denville, NJ 07834
(201) 328-4477
(201) 267-1444

Prophetic/Teaching Ministry
The Master's Place
Ministries Inc.
Bruce Hampton, Founder
Offering: prophetic teaching and
discreet ministerial credentials.
604 First Ave.
Alpena, MI 49707
(517) 356-1319

Seminars
Journey Toward
Wholeness Ministry
Don and Helen Crossland
P.O. Box 1019
N. Little Rock, AR 72115-1019
(501) 834-8908
(501) 834-8910 (FAX)

Other Ministry
Calvary Commission
Basic Christian Training School
P.O. Box 100
Lindale, TX 75771
(903) 882-5501

Christ Encounter Ministry, Inc.
Norm & Donna Tracy, Directors
22601 Pine Canyon Rd.
Tehachapi, CA 93561
(805) 822-7078

Mahesh Chavda Ministries Int'l.
P.O. Box 472009
Charlotte, N.C. 28247-2009
(704) 543-7272
(704) 541-5300 (FAX)

"Messianic Minutes"
Radio Outreach
"Time for the Church to Reach the
Lost Sheep of the House of Israel"
Teri Heger
P.O. Box 4006
Frederick, MD 21701
(301) 695-4496
(301) 662-1042 (FAX)

Spiritual Warfare Ministries, Inc.
Don Rogers, Director
P.O. Box 396
Warrington, PA 18976-0396
(215) 343-6474

Women's Ministry
Eagles Dare-NBFC Ministries
J.R. Luke, Director
Linda Fields, Asst.Director
P. O. Box 560
301 Sante Fe St.
Wolfe City, TX 75496
(903) 496-7376

Ministry Schools

I.M.I Bible College & Seminary
(Accredited Home Study & Exten-
sion Centers)
Dr. Mary A. Bruno, Founder/Pres.
P.O. Box 2107
Vista, CA 92085-2107
(619) 471-9390, 727-3998

International Children's
Ministry Institute
& School of the Spirit
P.O. Box 250
Litchfied, IL 62056
(217) 324-6215l

One Life Ministries
"Training the Church to Heal the
Wounded" --Tapes, seminars,
classes, & retreats
Ken Unger, Director
8740 Arborhurst Lane
Kirtland, OH 44094
(216) 256-1597

Stockholm Vineyard
School of Ministry
Hans Sundberg
Drottningholmsv 515
S-161 51 Bromma
Sweden
46-8 621 0022, FAX 364 080

MISSIONS

Africa Missions
Don and Cheri Crum
P.O. Box 1627
Lindale, TX 75771
(903) 963-5142
(903) 963-5748 (FAX)

Latter Rain Ministries, Inc.
Gwen Davis, Director
P.O. Box 250
Litchfield, IL 62056
(217) 324-62151

Reboboth Missions
Vincent Salazar, Director
Ostergade 39
7620 Lemvig
Denmark
(011 45) 9782-3056

**Your Missionary Outreach
of The Missionary Church
International**
Benjamin H. Covington, Bishop
P.O. Box 1761
Columbia, SC 29202
(803) 799-0502
(803) 254-7446 (FAX)

MUSIC

Starlight Studios
Leonard Jones, Chief Engineer
P.O. Box 369
Pineville, NC 28134

Pamela Morasch, M.Music
Piano music/praise & worship
teaching resources
Box 61091, Kensington P.O.
Calgary, Alberta Canada T2N 4S6

PRAYER NETWORK

Networking Intercessors
22 Harding Ave
Hatboro, PA 19040
(215) 675-6134

REAL ESTATE

Residential
John Joseph Davis, CSP
New Home Specialist
Relocations & Referrals
Coldwell Banker
(404) 565-9942

**Michael Zombo,
Property Specialist**
Coldwell Banker Professionals Inc.
761 Old Hickory Blvd., Suite 300
Brentewood, TN 37027
(615) 370-0766 (BUS.)
(615) 373-5261 (FAX)
(615) 395-4516 (RES.)

*Greensboro/High Point, NC
& National Relocation*
Ginny Forestieri, Realtor
Coldwell Banker/Jim Joyner Assoc.
1400 Battleground Ave., Suite 164
Greensboro, NC 27408
(800) 235-5957 (BUS.)
(910) 812-3790 (RES.)

RETREATS/CAMPS

Canby Grove Conference Center
Keith Johnson, Director
7501 Knights Bridge Rd.
Canby, OR 97013
(503) 266-5176
(503) 266-9970 (FAX)

TAPE SUPPLIES

Record Life Tape Supplies
David Roch
Box 54053 Village Sq PO
Calgary, AB
Canada T1Y 6S6
(403) 293-7150
(403) 280-6894 (FAX)

TELEPHONE SERVICE
WHOLESALE
LONG DISTANCE

**BNC Wholesale Long Distance
Telecommunications**
Chris J. Friberg, Indep. Rep.
2567 Elden Ave, Suite C 1
Costa Mesa, CA 92627
(714) 548-8979

TELEVISION STATIONS

KDOR TV 17
(Video production, training,
and helps available.)
Thomas Harrison, General Mgr.
2120 N. Yellowood
Broken Arrow, OK 74012
(918) 250-0777

TRAVEL SERVICES

TRAVISA Visa Services
Passports and foreign travel visas
2122 P Street NW
Washington, DC 20037
(800) 742-2796

T-Shirts/
Screen Printing

International Designs, Inc.
Martha or Vince Hoover
802 Coleman Blvd., Suite E
Mt. Pleasant, SC 29464
(803) 881-6525
(803) 884-6665 (FAX)

VETERINARIAN

Holistic Veterinary Services
Phone consultations available—
Call for cost and appointment.
(508) 521-1899
(508) 521-5297 (FAX)
Book—Natural Pet Care
Roger L. DeHaan, DVM, MTS
531 Amesbury Rd.
Havenhill, MA 01830

WALL PAPERING

Kingdom Wall Coverings
Blair Gravens
Residential/Commercial Installation
5327 Rita Kay Lane
Fort Worth, TX 76119
(817) 535-4473